Small Boat Sailing

COLLINS NUTSHELL BOOKS

Small Boat Sailing

COMMANDER D. A. RAYNER
D.S.C.*, V.R.D.

With Photographs and Diagrams

COLLINS
LONDON AND GLASGOW

First published 1962
Latest Reprint 1971

ISBN 0 00 411503 1

© *William Collins Sons & Co. Ltd., 1962*

PRINTED IN GREAT BRITAIN
BY COLLINS CLEAR-TYPE PRESS

Contents

CONTENTS

CONTENTS

AUTHOR'S NOTE

There is so much that could be written about this sailing game that it was difficult to decide how much to put into this book and yet keep it within the terms of reference which the publishers had set—a beginner's book.

In an effort to find the answer I went away in my own yacht to a secluded harbour taking with me a friend who, for all practical purposes, was a novice, and taking with us a fourteen-foot open sailing boat. From the answers to his many questions, and from the practical demonstrations he needed, this book has been built.

But it soon became obvious (on account of the permitted length) that we had to make a choice between dealing fully with a restricted target or more sketchily with a greater range. Now that it is finished I am sure that we have been right to limit ourselves to the needs of real beginners wishing to sail or motor such boats as can be car-topped or trailed to the water for use as day sailers. The matter of cruising in larger yachts calls for another volume which I trust the publishers will allow me to write one day.

Yacht *Orchid*.
Off Buckler's Hard in the Beaulieu River.

CHAPTER 1

The basic rules of sailing can be learnt from a book—What sort of boat do you want?—The first cost of a boat is not all the expense necessary before a ship is ready for sea—This expense expressed as a percentage of first cost—Yearly upkeep as a percentage of capital outlay—Choice of the boat will depend on your temperament—And even then must be a compromise.

To be forced to learn from one's own experience can be very costly: to learn by the experience of others may often leave an unpleasant taste (for no one who really likes boats can bear to see them hurt or wilfully mishandled), and so to gain instruction from a book will for many be both the easiest and the safest way of preparing to go afloat.

In many endeavours connected with the outside world the older practitioners of the art have for so long maintained " you can't learn it from books " that this dictum has passed into our corporate consciousness as a truism which often goes unchallenged. But who would expect an engineer, a doctor or any of the new technologists to acquire their knowledge without recourse to the library? The plain fact is that you *can* find your basic knowledge in a book. You can learn enough to venture forth unaided as it were " upon the nursery slopes."

And this is just as it should be—for the novice will learn more quickly by doing so—but only for so long as he remains conscious of his current standard of proficiency. With whatever distinction a doctor may pass into his profession he is still expected to go through a period of post-examinational training amongst experienced practical men before he is let out on his own. So it must be with the seaman. Whatever his theoretical knowledge may be, he will become a danger to himself and to others if he tries to progress too fast and make passages beyond his experience. It is with the hope of producing a sound and balanced approach to this business of going about in boats that this book is written.

The first thing to decide is what sort of boat you want, either in which to learn or ultimately own, for the two may not necessarily be the same. It is quite reasonable to buy a small boat which can be trailed home, to gain experience of how to handle boats in general, while you decide on the locality which is best suited to your home and business.

The choice of boat will depend on many things; your pocket; your ultimate purpose—racing, cruising or family pottering (boats provide such an infinite variety of pleasures!); whether you must take her home after every sail or only for the winter; the number of people you would like to, or must, take with you. In fact the demands that each one of us will make on our boats are so varied that it is not too much to say that, ideally, each and every boat should be tailor-made to suit the needs of her owner. And indeed this is pretty well what did happen until only a few years ago. In the days when a man went down to the small builder whose yard was a time-worn shed where the lane petered out on a pebble beach he did just that— and had to pay for his privilege. In those days, and I speak of a period only just before the second World War, the owning of a boat was considered quite beyond the general public.

Happily those days are gone and now, in modern factories with all the appearance of big business, splendid little boats are built by the thousand for the nation's pleasure and profit. I make no apology for the use of the last word, indeed I would blazon it out in letters of fire

10

against an ink-black sky—BOATS ARE GOOD FOR YOU—and they are. In my not so very long life I have seen so many children led to responsible manhood in little hulls, I've seen many fretted workers calmed and made fit by a few days under the slim white sails, marriages held together, businesses saved, in fact I have yet to meet a family which has not benefited by its venture into boats. But that remark holds good only for so long as no accident is allowed to mar the owning of a boat.

The sea or any other water, even the most placid, is a greedy beast once it is more than chin deep. It is a fact which must never be forgotten, however difficult it may be when sailing easily over the sunlit waves to remember that your little ship is in reality nothing but a small scallop-shaped platform suspended many feet above the earth; no more than the basket hung below a balloon. With your new boat must go adequate safety, and in one respect at least safety means more money paid out.

So many people contemplating the purchase of a boat will consider only the first cost of the hull and disregard the money that must necessarily be laid out before their little ship is a safe one in which to go to sea. I think it is a reasonable suggestion—for in this connection no comment is worth making unless a figure be attempted—that the cost of fitting out a boat with anchor, cable, fenders, mooring ropes and personal buoyancy will be about 10% of her first cost in the case of a day-sailing boat but may well be nearer 30% in the case of a small cruiser needing, in addition to the items listed above, a set of moorings, a dinghy, compass, wireless, charts and more varied ground-tackle. The point made at the moment is that all the available money should not be spent on the boat; that the ancillary equipment must be considered; that insurance (at about 35/- per cent) will be an absolute necessity.

11

These percentages apply to new boats. A boat bought at second-hand is unlikely to be sold along with any of the gear that these percentage figures have been assumed to cover. Even if she be cheaper in first cost the price of fitting her out will be the same as that of her younger sister—and the percentage will then be very much larger. It is a point not always remembered.

The intending owner should look forward into the future and try to assess the cost of yearly upkeep. However desirable it may be to own a boat for family happiness and health it is obviously absurd to risk the introduction of an incubus which will be too great a drain on the family or the personal income. Better to cut the size and the cost of the boat to that which can be maintained without strain.

Here again, to have any validity figures must be mentioned. My own records show that the cost of upkeep is quite remarkably close to a steady 10% of capital cost. This has been exceeded only when I have owned old boats which needed a deal of repair. So, when considering second-hand boats, the percentage must be based on the first cost of that type of boat, and not on the amount you may have actually paid. This 10% for upkeep refers to boats of what we might call traditional construction. Plywood boats with their few joints, boats of cold-moulded ply with their almost one-piece hulls, and boats of fibre-glass will, in this order, cost progressively less to maintain (say 7%, 6% and 3%). But if their maintenance is less we have to remember that, except in the case of the fibre-glass boat, a major repair may well be much more difficult and costly than with any of the older methods of construction. The fibre-glass boat scores heavily in this respect. In fact it scores heavily all along the line. Easily repaired ashore, its one disadvantage is the greater apparent difficulty of effecting emergency repairs in the case of damage suffered when actually at sea. I use the word " apparent " because many people think it cannot be done. This is not so; it can be repaired quite easily, and how to do so will be described in chapter 3.

With the limits imposed by cost and geographical situation goes the limit fixed by the temperament of the intending purchaser. It has to be remembered that a boat, however perfect her design may be, is no better than her crew makes her, and the fact is that men tire or fall into exhaustion at vastly different rates for any given set of physical conditions: that fear (which may or may not result from inexperience) is the greatest single sapper of strength: that some boats are much harder on their crews than others and so must be supposed to impose more strain and reduce the period during which their men can remain efficient.

It will be seen then that the real temperament of the owner is going to make a deal of difference to his choice: that many boats soon placed on the second-hand market are only there because they have not suited the man who bought on sales-chatter and without thought of what would really suit him. Within the white walls of the showroom a racing dinghy may look a sound enough job and appear to be a docile enough creature when handled expertly by her yellow-smocked crew on a sunlit day. But the same boat can be a devil incarnate when manned by the novice, his wife and his ten-year-old child.

In no other field of sport is the price of over-bidding one's personal capabilities quite so high. The true artist functions within the limits of the capacity of himself and his ship. To go beyond this would be, for him, bad art. Neither the sea nor ships will put up with this. Their retribution is desperately swift and can often be pushed to the point of extinction. Boats cannot be bluffed by a show of either wealth or power. Perhaps in this lies the great

13

attraction of sailing and its peculiar hold on our nation. Before the sea we are all equal.

And it *is* an attractive sport: one which can bring pleasure to all the members of the family. It is not the prerogative of any one age-group, and increasing years do not lessen one's pleasure or profit from the enterprise. Indeed I have never met anyone who proposed to know much about it who would not, however hoary his head, have admitted that he had still a great deal to learn.

Do not be dismayed by the apparent contradictions of this introductory chapter. They have been put before you for the specific purpose of pointing out that the choice of boat is worth a great deal of thought: that the decision when made is almost certain to be a compromise, and that the sea is not to be trifled with.

I often hear it said that there are already too many boats. This I do not and will not believe. The sea is a mighty big place and there is plenty of room for all of us. Maybe the rivers and estuaries appear to be becoming a little overcrowded. But do not worry. If they do become so the local authorities will be forced to do something about it and provide the facilities that the public need. If they won't, then you may be sure that private enterprise will.

It is intended in the following chapters to discuss in some detail the various constructions, materials and hull forms, to give enough instruction to enable you to get away from the beach in your own boat, and when you get to the end of that, my friend, you should have made up *your* mind on the sort of boat *you* want—and good luck to you.

CHAPTER 2

The choice of cruising grounds and where to keep the boat—At home, in a club compound or on moorings?—The natural stability of the hull will vary with the type of boat the designer planned—The boat for the child beginner—And for the family—How the stability of a hull may be known—The road trailer.

Before we tackle the business of going to sea it will be worth while to decide what sort of boat you are going to have so that the later chapters will speak more clearly to you.

First, then, there is the question of where the boat will be kept during the periods when you cannot use her. There are really only three ways of keeping a boat: either on moorings, in the club dinghy park, or on a trailer in the garden. The choice will depend to a large extent on where you live in relation to the harbour from which you sail. Both mooring a boat and keeping her at the club will restrict your operations to one particular anchorage, but with a trailer you can, in theory, go wherever you like and put your boat in the water.

This last way sounds an ideal solution, but unfortunately it is not quite so easily put into practice. The roads are often crowded, and it is (I know, for my business demands that I do much towing) a great deal more tiring to drive a car when there is a boat behind. Rest and relaxation are what we seek and so I feel it is a poor end to a good day if the drive home with a boat takes more than an hour; for even when the police are not in evidence I find it difficult to average much more than the 30 miles an hour allowed by the law.

Then again, the untended slipways are often highly

dependent on the height of the tide, their lower slopes are deep in mud, the middle portion is covered with green weed on which the back tyres of your car spin like Catherine Wheels, while the top of the slip will be jammed with parked vehicles.

Choice would again seem to be determined by temperament. For myself I find the almost hourly change in weather sufficient to dispel the apparent monotony of using the same sailing ground week after week—for when has one ever known the sea to be the same on one day as on another? Then, too, there is the advantage of human contacts made. There is something warming to the heart when you are recognised in the local shop and in the pub. Week-end friendships are formed and a separate holiday society built up into which you can escape from the everyday world.

Moorings must be properly layed by a competent man under the authority of the local harbour master. It should cost between £10 and £15 to collect the chain, sinkers, swivel and the buoy which will be necessary, and there may or may not be a yearly rental charge by the local authority. Even if this is not likely to exceed three or four pounds for the size of boat with which this book deals, it is not the end of the expense of the moorings. A small boat left on moorings is very vulnerable to weather and must have someone to keep an eye on her, to pump her out and to watch for chafe. Local boatmen can be expected to charge between five and ten shillings a week for this service. For myself I would say that this is not a subject for economy. These worthy men are as human as everyone else and so if you want good service you have to pay a reasonable price for it. The modern boatman must have a motor-boat to get round his many charges. Petrol costs money, and a small open boat may well be a greater call on a man's time than a fully-decked yacht.

There is another problem with mooring small boats. Most of these of the size we are discussing will have been more or less mass-produced and, being so, will be open for price comparison, one boat against another. Now the many little price-wars inherent in our present society have one great benefit and one major disadvantage. If they keep down the price of the article and enforce business efficiency on the manufacturer, they also prevent the conscientious builder, who tries to put as much quality into the hull as he can, from giving his boat anything but the very minimum of fittings—otherwise he will price his product out of the market. Most builders, myself included, have to assume that their small sailing boats will be hauled up in club enclosures and will be tied to pontoons or catamarans only for very short periods. It follows that the bow-fittings which are supplied are quite inadequate for securing to a mooring in open water. A strong cleat on the foredeck is needed (or better still, if the mast is left stepped, a strop can be put round the mast to which a hook is fastened) and then some form of strong metal bow-fitting in which the mooring rope can lie without being chafed must be found. Fig. 1 shows the arrangement which should be arrived at.

All in all, I think it best to keep the boat in a club enclosure during the summer and take her home for the winter. This will simplify the matter of buying a trailer; for the type which will serve for launching down a club slipway is vastly cheaper than the one necessary for road transport, and at that time of the year you may well be able to borrow a road trailer for the journey or have the boat taken home on a lorry. Working from a club has the great advantage of meeting people with similar interests and of having people about who will offer assistance when you need it.

Now, having made up your mind as to where and how

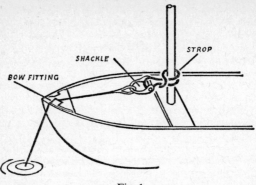

Fig. 1

the boat is to be kept, you can proceed to the selection of the boat itself. This is a problem which must be tackled in two parts: the type of boat that will suit you, and the material from which she had best be built.

The novice is unlikely to derive complete satisfaction from a boat designed for the experienced dinghy sailor. And, if the word " novice " be considered and analysed, we shall find that we have to look for a difference between the boat which will suit the child starter and the one which we would choose for the man or woman who takes up the sport in maturity. If both have the need to learn the same basic principles, the type of boat that each will ask for will be completely different in size and cost. And yet both, if they are not to be scared out of their wits and driven from the sport in the first few days, will have the same crying need—a really stable hull.

The natural stability of a hull is the compound of two qualities, shape and weight. By shape alone a designer

18

can give a boat enormous stability. Weight, either as ballast or the movable weight of the crew, can enhance this natural stability—which is just as it should be. But, and this is a big " but," the ballast or crew weight in very fast boats can be used to replace much of the natural stability that could have been built into a given hull. It happens, then, that many such boats, designed to be raced by agile crews who sit on the gunwale and lean out until their bodies are only a few inches from the waves, are of much less stable hull form than their more sedate sisters.

Racing is a different form of the same sport, and one which cannot be recommended to our sort of beginner, certainly not if he is to make his first venture by himself. The way into this sort of sailing is different. You must first crew for someone else and then, after a season's experience, you may be ready for your own fast boat. The snag with this advice is that, as happened to me when I first started, all the good skippers in the class were adequately provided with crews and the only one I could find to take me proved to be the most ham-fisted man with whom I have ever sailed! He actually succeeded in scaring me so much that I preferred to do my own frightening and so, half way through the season, bought a boat of my own. Which, if it belies my own advice, still does, I think, leave the advice valid.

But to return to the matter under discussion, the shape of the hull. If you walk along any sea-front where dinghies and other small craft are parked you will see boats whose midship section will vary from the completely flat-floored box to the half circle. The former is the most, and the latter is the least, inherently stable. But observe that, whereas the stability of the flat-floored craft may be extreme to start with, there will come a point where she may be capsized—and this she will do if pressed beyond her stability, without warning and with great swiftness. At the other end of the scale the hull of the half-circular form will retain the stability given her by the out-sitting weight of her crew through all angles of heel until the water pours over the gunwale, when she will prefer to fill and sink on her side rather than turn over.

Now the weight of the crew (if proportionate to the size of the boat) will, if allied to the flat-floored craft, make a boat so stiff that it can safely be recommended for the child beginner. In fact I can think of no craft more suitable for this purpose than the small flat-floored pram dinghy with a dagger plate and a simple rig. It is I think, absolutely essential that *all* a child's efforts should be devoted to tillering his craft and trimming his sails. It will detract from his pleasure if the rig is complicated and finicky, needing many little turnbuckles and shackles to hold it together. It is essential, too, that this first boat should be well designed and a good performer. Nothing can be more disheartening for a child than a boat that will not sail.

Those starting to sail in maturity will need a larger boat and may well wish to carry a family along with them. While a blown-up version of the child's boat is a possible solution, there is no getting away from the fact that she would be an unlovely craft. As such a person will want a boat whose appearance is in keeping with his car and his house, some cross between the two extremes must be found—some hull which will be beautiful as well as stable. Fortunately this is possible. It is quite easy to design an adequately fast boat which will not call for her people to sit on the gunwale to keep her on her feet. The crew must, of course, be prepared to change sides when she is put from one tack to the other—but this, I think, should be the limit of activity required of them.

Such a boat can be recognised on sight if you know

what to look for and where to find it. Being an unballasted craft, its stability is governed by a simple geometrical problem. Fig. 2 is the mid-section of such a boat. AB is the waterline passing the centreline of the boat at O. Now if we assume the boat to have been heeled through 10 degrees, we get a new waterline CD, and the unshaded

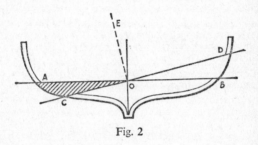

Fig. 2

portion DOB will represent that part of the boat which goes into the water as she heels, and AOC will be that portion which comes out. But the two wedges are not equal in size. In fact as the boat heels she will try to put a great deal more of herself in the water than she takes out. It is, of course, impossible for her to increase draught in this way. What happens is that she will try to rise in the water: a rise which is countered by her own weight and by the weight of all the crew within the boat so long as they are anywhere between A and O, and to windward of the line OE. In other words, her weight and disposal of the weight of the crew act together to give her the required stability.

We have considered only the mid-section. If you look again at fig. 2 and imagine the bow, you will see that there the " in and out wedges " are more dissimilar than at mid-section, and then, going to the other end and considering the stern, the difference is even greater for here such a hull will be flatter and approximate more closely to the box than the cigar.

This is not to suggest that by corollary all semi-circular boats are bad ones. Although such a hull form is less stable than the one we have suggested, and relies on the weight of its crew to stay upright, it is almost certainly faster. But then I do seriously suggest that the ultra fast boat is not the one for a beginner. Such hulls, termed " log-rollers " from the similarity of their behaviour to that of a log in the water, do require expert handling; as does that other type of craft which is equally unsuitable for the novice—the very shallow flat-floored craft with a tall and pressing Bermudan rig. Such a boat, which will have great initial stability, can, if sailed hard, capsize with great suddenness. And the question of " sailing hard " is not one that is always within the control of the helmsman. Wind velocity is most variable and so, whatever one's intention and whatever sail one may have chosen to carry, the days which do not provide a surprise gesture by the wind are few indeed.

Stability is often thought of as a product of beam. But this is by no means necessarily so. Stability can be obtained by added length without any increase in beam. In fact with boats built of traditional materials it can be said, taking the world as a whole, that heavy boats are short (and broad or deep) while light boats tend to be long and narrow. Look at fig. 3. If we express the difference between the " in " wedges and the " out " as an area ABCD it would represent the natural righting moment of the hull. Now if that hull is increased in length from C to F we see that we have added a righting moment equal to the parallelogram CDFG.

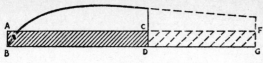

Fig. 3

What help have we now got for the family man wishing to buy his first boat? That the boat should be of a good stable midship section which can be sailed in all reasonable weather by his crew sitting on seats along and within the boat's side and without their having to lean out over the gunwale: that, consistent with the weight that can be handled on to a trailer, the boat should be as long as possible (which will put her somewhere between 14 and 15 feet): that lastly, although by no means the least important, she should be beautiful. Of what material she should be built we can leave to another chapter, and the question of rig to yet another.

To close this chapter we can discuss the road trailer which will be necessary if your decision has been that the boat be taken daily to the water. Many marine dealers have told me that there is more sales-resistance to the purchase of a trailer than to the boat itself, and assure me that most men will rather pay £50 more for a slightly better boat than an extra £10 for a much better trailer. Now this is absurd; for the difference in pleasure between handling and towing a reliable trailer is worth a great deal more, to say nothing of the relief from worry about burst tyres, worn bearings, and tail-wag on the road.

A good trailer should have six-ply tyres, sealed hubs fitted with grease nipples and the weight on the draw bar with the boat in the travelling position should be between 56 and 84 lbs. But, as this weight may be too heavy for some people to lift as they wheel-barrow the boat over ground which will not always be concrete, the draw-bar end of the trailer should have a jockey wheel, either detachable or mounted on a telescopic tube. Even if a jockey wheel is not thought to be necessary, a skeg should be fitted to keep the draw bar attachment off the ground; for if pebbles or mud are allowed to work their way into the ball socket a false-marriage may result and the trailer may come unhitched on the road. Remember that, contrary to what one might think, tyres are less likely to overheat if the pressure, consistent with the weight of the boat, is kept high—45 lbs. as a minimum and 60 lbs. as a maximum.

CHAPTER 3

The various methods of building—Notes on the following:—
clinker, carvel, marine ply, hot and cold moulded ply, metal, fibre-
glass—The relative weight of the various constructions; prices and
cost of upkeep.

Before attempting to draw any general conclusions on
the choice of material and the method of construction it
would be as well to run through the various methods of
building.

Many people think that the clinker (or lap-strake)
construction is the oldest. But it seems that this is not so.
The earliest boats had sides built up of planks thonged to
the edge of the hollowed-out log which was the basic part
of the boat and, as boats grew larger when iron was able
to help hollow out a larger log, ribs were put in to hold the
deeper plank.

From this conjunction of the keel to the sides, boats
developed in two ways—clinker, where the edges of the
planks overlapped each other, and carvel, where the edges
butted against the plank on either side and in which seams
were caulked with waterproof materials.

Fig. 4 is the section of a carvel-built boat and fig. 5 that
of a clinker boat. The advantages and disadvantages of
these two types must for thousands of years have been a
constant source of discussion between small-boat sailors
and one can well imagine Peter and Our Lord arguing
this particular toss (which by then was already an old one)
as their boat lay becalmed on the Sea of Galilee. But
whatever the result of such an apochryphal discussion
may have been, the seamen of the world seem to have
decided that carvel was better for the heavier boat while

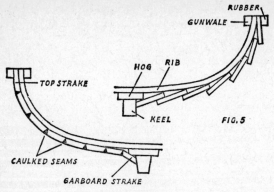

Figs. 4 and 5

clinker was best suited to the lighter craft. From our present-day point of view, and so long as our interest is centred on the boat under 18 feet in length, the situation is at once complicated by the appearance of new materials or new methods of construction. Clinker and carvel are both unsuited to boats which are put on a trailer and kept out of the water for long periods. The planks will shrink and then, when they are put back in the water, they will leak.

Both are quite suitable for craft kept permanently in the water. The clinker construction, with the laps of the planks riveted together, is very strong and the best suited for boats that are hauled up every night and run down on the next day, i.e. for the use of coastal fishermen and for the dinghies of cruising yachts in temperate climes.

For the life that is lived by a trailed boat it is necessary to choose some method of construction which will remain

26

watertight even if the boat is kept out of the water in hot dry weather for long periods. This demands a hull which, if it be wood, is stuck together with adhesives as well as being fastened. The simplest and cheapest of these new methods is sheets of marine plywood glued to the hog and the chines.

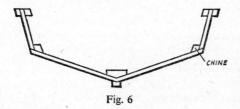

Fig. 6

Fig. 6 is the typical mid-section of such a craft, and at once its simple shape draws attention to the main disadvantage of the type if it is not to become almost as complicated and expensive to build as a traditional hull. The ply sheets will bend readily only in the fore and aft direction. With care in design and some trouble in manufacture, which means added cost, ply can be induced to take up a transverse curve to the extent of one inch of curve in every 12 inches of span, but few builders seem to do so and boats of this construction are generally flat-sided.

One might wonder how, from the design point of view, such a hull can be made to comply with our decision in the previous chapter about the in and out wedges. But, as you will see from the pecked line on the right side of fig. 7, a pretty fair attempt can be made even with a single chine boat, while an even closer approximation can be obtained if two chines are used as I have shown on the left side of fig. 7.

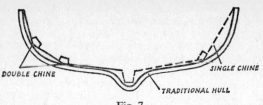

DOUBLE CHINE

SINGLE CHINE

TRADITIONAL HULL

Fig. 7

Good marine ply is, as far as we yet know, almost immune from ageing, but it must be said that not all the ply that is about is of the best quality. The British Standards specification 1088 refers only to the bonding material to be used and not to the wood. Quite a number of the earlier plys were made with core woods of too soft a type, and some still are. There is no way, once the wood has been fastened, of seeing what the core (the inner layer) may be. Only the builder's reputation can guarantee the use of the best wood. Fortunately, most builders are responsible people and build boats because they love them. Boats from good yards are very unlikely to be built in anything but the best materials.

For small repairs to the hull (up to 6 in. × 6 in.) pieces of ply can be scarfed in so that they are invisible, even if to do so is a job for the professional. Plywood will in fact hold screws better than it would appear to do and in an emergency a patch can be screwed over the damaged part in a matter of minutes and can be expected to hold until a proper repair is effected. For larger areas of damage the matter is more serious for if the ply has to be cleaned off any part of the framing of the boat the wood will part before the glue seam which means that the frame itself will also have to be re-surfaced. In fact, it is probably an uneconomic proposition to try to repair a badly damaged small plywood boat. This is a fact which has to be faced.

The same applies in principle to boats of cold or hot moulded ply. In this construction it is unfortunate that the word ply has come to be used for this method of building because it would have been more accurate to use the word " veneer." In this construction thin layers of veneer are built up diagonally to the centre line, each layer being about three inches wide. Two, and sometimes three, skins are thus bonded together with a phenolic resin and the whole boat is thereby formed into one leak-proof structure.

As far as repair is concerned the same remarks apply to this construction as to the ordinary hard-chine plywood hull, and if there is any other criticism it is only on the score of hull shape, which in this type of building is limited by the natural curve of the wood veneer. It follows that the designer will be very restricted by his medium in the smaller sizes of boats, where the curves are more acute. Such designs tend to be bluff, almost spoon, bowed. In the larger boats (above fourteen feet) this disadvantage can to a great extent be overcome.

Metal boats, although temporarily popular as an off-shoot of the wartime aeroplane industry before the wood-workers got into their peacetime stride, are not often seen as sailing boats. The use of this material is more often found in the high-speed motor-boat to which it seems to be more aesthetically suited. For this use it has many advantages, of which strength and easily-framed rigidity are probably the most important. As a disadvantage, it dents easily and does not hold paint as well as a hull of wood, while repairs really need the attention of an expert metal-worker—not always easily found along the coast.

29

The last type of construction to be considered, and the most difficult to deal with in a short treatise, is fibre-glass. This is the newest product, and when it is really good it is by far the best in which to build the sort of hull we are discussing. When such a boat is built of first-class material, with the use of the proper resins and by expert workmen, I am sure there is no other material which can so nearly offer the public the perfect boat. The past trouble with fibre-glass has been twofold—bad construction in building down to a price, and the high cost of the initial mould which has deterred the builders (often without any previous connection with the sea and boats) from adding to their overhead costs the fees of a really good designer and the royalty that would be his due.

The result of such an approach is obvious. " Crazing " hulls and unstable craft gave the early products a bad name. But now I think the tide is changing. Despite the unscrupulous manufacturer, fibre-glass is coming into its own and there are a number of first-class hulls on the market which can be expected to give their owners years of untroubled service.

The product has many advantages to the designer, the builder and the owner. The architect is not restricted in his design by any of the properties of the product he is handling. The only desideratum is that the hull should be able to be lifted from the mould without " locking in." And even so, if it were sufficiently desirable to incorporate some particular feature (say a big tumble-home of the topsides) which would cause the hull to " lock," each side of the hull can be built in separate moulds and then joined up down the centre line.

From the builder's point of view, he gets a hull which he knows will give no trouble to his customer—but only for so long as he employs expert workmen of great integrity. For the fact is that the apparently messy business of laying up a fibre-glass hull demands the most exact attention to the minutest detail, because the resin has to be worked and worked through the mat until absolutely the last vestige of an air bubble has been rolled out.

A good hull should be made from high density mat, with a flexible resin and the mix should not contain more than 8% of inert filler. In this respect, too, one can see a fundamental error being introduced by advertising agents who cry " no fillers used," whereas the fact is that some filler is an absolute necessity if maximum strength and impact resistance is to be obtained. The point is that many early boats were turned out with the filler content, for the sake of cheapness, raised to as much as 60%, which caused severe embrittlement as the boat aged.

If properly built, a fibre-glass hull will take incredible shocks without " crazing " the outer or " gel " coat film. It can quickly be polished up to " mint " condition, never needs painting, can very easily be supplied with built-in buoyancy (and normally is so fitted), is completely leak-proof, quite immune to marine borers, and the hull if submitted to the Izod test will prove to be more than twice as strong (even though the hull thickness is less than half) as that of a wooden boat of comparable length.

Major repairs to a fibre-glass hull are probably more easily, more cheaply, and much more speedily made than to either of the other materials. But, to effect a good repair, the surface must be *absolutely* dry. This makes impossible the emergency repair of such a hull by the usually employed " build-up " method. The only way of making a temporary repair at sea would be to have some sheets of 1/16 in. fibre-glass material made up with a heavily plasticised resin. These thin sheets, easily bent to the curve of a hull, could then be used as a copper tingle is used to repair a wooden boat and can be held in place by self-tapping screws, which hold well in fibre-glass.

The only disadvantages are that a properly built fibre-glass hull will be between 10% and 20% more expensive than a wooden hull of the same size, and about the same percentage heavier. Buoyancy, even though it takes up less room because of the ease of fitting the tanks, must be greater than in the case of a wooden boat, for where one of wood will probably support its own weight when filled, a boat of fibre-glass must be a dead weight all the time. It is a point one has often seen overlooked.

To sum up a chapter such as this I propose to give a table of relative weights, costs (with sails), and yearly maintenance of the various constructions of trailerable boats, assuming a fourteen-foot long sailing hull. I do so with some trepidation because, although much is a compound of the advertising material of other manufacturers, a great deal is only from my own head and must therefore be regarded as personal advice rather than provable fact: a remark which is particularly applicable to the line for "Yearly Upkeep" where I have costed personal labour as if it had to be payed for were the boat to be handed over to a yard for refit. But here, surely, hardly anyone would put a fibre-glass boat out when the man-hours for maintenance are so few.

	Hard Chine Marine Ply	Moulded Veneer	Fibre-Glass
WEIGHT	270 lbs.	260 lbs.	335 lbs.
COST	£215	£250	£260
YEARLY UPKEEP	£20	£25	£5

Lastly, just one point applicable to the boat for the child beginner. I have seen my own young let loose with a varnish brush and the consequent tears as a result of the

The *National Enterprise* 13 ft. 3 ins. day boat/racing dinghy. Originally sponsored by the " News Chronicle " and designed by Jack Holt, this has been one of the most successful post-war small boats. (*Photo. Eileen Ramsay.*)

The " *Yachting World* " *G.P.14*. Another extremely popular Jack Holt design. Even if the accent of this 14-foot boat is more on racing than day sailing, she will prove an excellent day boat in experienced hands. (*Photo. Eileen Ramsay.*)

finished article being a long way from the smooth job which childish imagination had painted. I have trodden in spilled varnish and then walked through the house. I have found my best brush a hard relic of its former supple self. All the foregoing woes have ended in my having to do the boat myself, and so I would have no hesitation in recommending the fibre-glass boat for the child even if it were not for its last unmatchable point ; that real unsinkable buoyancy can be built in and my children's lives do not depend on punctureable bags tied in with webbing straps.

CHAPTER 4

Rigs—The parts of a sail—The cloths from which sails are made—
The stretching of cotton sails—Synthetic fibres not immune from
all troubles—Mildew can attack Terylene and chafe may be worse
with the new material—How the sails drive a boat—The lessons to
be learnt from the diagrams—The work done by the jib—The need
for battens in the mainsail, and sometimes in the jib too.

The sails of a boat are worth a deal of your consideration
when deciding on the craft which is most fitted to your
needs, and reorganisation of a sail plan can turn a boat
which previously had been unsafe for a novice into one
which is wholly desirable. This works both ways, and
there are many good hulls that have been made need-
lessly tricky to handle by a rig which is suited only to the
expert.

It seems to me that the majority of designers and
builders, aiming to catch the attention of the racing
yachtsman, neglect both the man who is starting and
the one who only wants a quiet sail with his family. The
Bermudan rig, particularly the modern sail of high aspect
ratio, is a very powerful sail and a very pressing one
indeed. It is a sail without " life " and " lift," driving
the boat through the seas rather than helping her to fly
over them.

Those of us who, before the motor-boat became
ubiquitous, were privileged to sail in the big open boats of
the Navy, remember the enormous lifting power of the big
loose-footed lugsails. As a method of harnessing the
power of the wind without depressing the lee gunwale
beyond reason they were supremely efficient, with the
certainty that, when it did blow too hard for the sail you

34

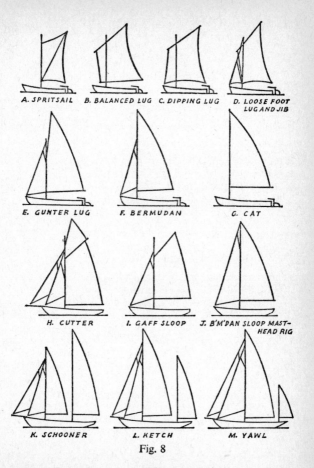

A. SPRITSAIL   B. BALANCED LUG   C. DIPPING LUG   D. LOOSE FOOT LUG AND JIB

E. GUNTER LUG   F. BERMUDAN   G. CAT

H. CUTTER   I. GAFF SLOOP   J. B'M'DAN SLOOP MAST-HEAD RIG

K. SCHOONER   L. KETCH   M. YAWL

Fig. 8

were carrying, the wind could quickly be spilled from the straining canvas. So too with the Deal luggers and the big two-masted fishing vessels known as Zulus which hailed from the Aberdeenshire coast. I find it difficult to believe that all these workboats were wrong or that the fishermen of Portugal and Ireland are likewise loose in the head.

I am not, you will note, saying that there is anything wrong with the Bermudan rig for the purpose of racing or when fitted to larger boats capable of standing up to the pressure it can exert. My point is that there are other rigs worthy of consideration and that a great many of these are safer for the boat, far less complicated, and allow of more latitude for any personal error. On the previous page, in fig. 8, I have set out illustrations of the twelve rigs most likely to be met with round our coasts. Types A, B, C, D and E are those suitable for small boats and the others are, generally speaking, for use by decked yachts. I propose to discuss the former and make only passing comment on the others.

Before we start talking about sails we must get the names of the parts right. Fig. 9 gives them all.

In comment on fig. 9 it is pointed out that the term " head " is applied to the top *corner* of a triangular sail whether it is a foresail or mainsail, but in the gaff sail or in the lug this term refers to a *side*. And again, when two headsails are used, as in the larger rigs, the inner sail (next the mast) is the foresail and the outer sail is called a jib. The rope that is sewn to the luff of the sail is called a luff-rope and the fine line that runs down the leach of many sails is called a leach-line: its use is to adjust the flow of the sail to the wind. Once properly adjusted so that the leach does not shake, it should not need to be altered except on rare occasions. The leach-line is assisted in its efforts to keep the sail flat by battens set in pockets

36

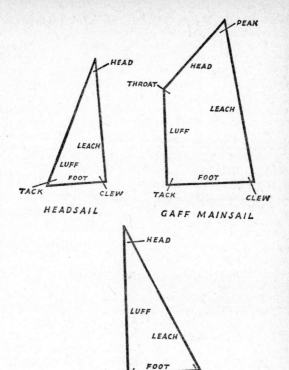

HEADSAIL

GAFF MAINSAIL

BERMUDAN MAINSAIL

Fig. 9

37

(three or four is the usual number). The upper battens should be set at right angles to the leach as they do their work more efficiently that way, but the lower batten (presuming the boat be fitted with roller reefing) should be parallel with the boom. If it is so, then there is no need to pause in the middle of what is always inclined to be a hectic operation in order to take it out. It can be allowed to roll up with the sail. It is a small point such as this which shows that the boat has been built by practical people. The eyelets in the corners of the sail are called " cringles."

First then, let us talk about the Sprit Sail, fig. 8A. This sail is the simplest of all and is no more than a sail held up by one diagonal yard or " sprit." The head of the pointed yard is pushed into a becket on the head of the sail while its heel, similarly pointed, is held in a snotter (loop of rope) passed round the mast and tucked into its own part to form an eye. See fig. 10.

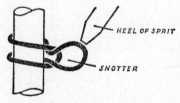

Fig. 10

The snotter can be pushed up the mast to tighten the rig and the only other ropes that are needed are a halyard to hoist the sail, a light line to lace the luff of the sail to the mast and a sheet to control the clew. This rig, because of its simplicity, is an extremely good rig for a child beginner because it contains so few bits and pieces, and because there are so few ropes in which the crew can become entangled in the event of a capsize. It is very easily spilled of wind, and yet, because of its breadth in relation to height, it has very good " drive " and plenty of " lift." It might be thought that it would set much better when the wind is blowing from the side of the sail on which the sprit stands than when the wind is blowing against the sprit. This however seems to be more in the imagination than apparent in action.

The next is fig. 8B, the Balanced Lug. This is an excellent little sail for a dinghy and was, until the early thirties of this century, the standard rig for the boat of nine to thirteen feet in length. It can be used with the sail laced to both the yard and the boom, or the sail can be set loose-footed and secured to the boom only by lashings at the tack and the clew. In this case the foot of the sail is cut in a downward sweeping curve called a " roach." It sets equally well on either tack. It is hoisted so that the halyard is close up to the sheave and then the fore-end of the boom is hauled down with a tack-tackle. (The second " tackle " is always pronounced tay-kle when it refers to a block and rope: Heaven alone knows why—presumably to avoid the phonetic repetition in the instance above!) I like this rig because when you let go the halyard the whole lot falls into the boat to lie below the gunwale, allowing oars to be got out at once if they are needed.

Fig. 8C, the Dipping Lug is not used much these days. It is loose-footed and a wonderful sail with which to go into deep water and a big sea. It probably gives a closer approximation to bird flight than any other sailing machine but it does imply the use of a big and trained crew as the yard must be dipped round the mast each time the boat goes about. First cousin to the traditional lateen rig of the Mediterranean and the dhows of the Indian Ocean, it was the rig of naval cutters and Deal luggers. Like all good rigs it can be dropped down and muzzled quickly. It is beautiful and exciting but not, I am afraid, really practical for small boat sailing.

Fig. 8D, the Loose-Footed Standing Lug, if properly cut and given a small jib, is in my opinion the best possible rig for the novice and the potterer. It has plenty of lift, can be dropped almost as fast as thought—certainly more quickly than the words take to write—and when it is down it too falls below the gunwale. For boats that are trailed, all the spars can be carried inside the hull, and when sailing there is no boom to crack the heads of those only recently initiated.

Fig. 8F, the Bermudan Rig, is the modern racing rig and, while it is certainly the most efficient to windward, it is just as certainly (because of its increased efficiency) the rig which for a given sail area is the most pressing. I do feel, however, that its advantages to windward, so important for racing, may well have resulted in its general efficiency being over-estimated, certainly so for the day sailer and the learner. In actual fact, when off the wind the rig is no faster, and may well be slower, than the same sail area in a form which has more lift. Moreover, the racing men have introduced a number of innovations which, though entirely suited to their own sport, are not necessarily compatible with good seamanship for the ordinary sailing boat.

As originally introduced the luff of the sail ran up the mast on a brass track to which it was held by travellers. And so it still is on all proper cruising yachts. It is, of course, undeniable that this allows a gap between the sail and the mast which may increase the wind eddies round the spar and reduce the aerodynamic efficiency of the sail. To overcome this the racing man, who only hoists his sail before the race and lowers it on return to the catamaran or launching site, devised a method of running the luff rope up a groove in the after side of the mast. The wind then runs more smoothly into the sail and this construction has the added advantage with built-up hollow wooden spars or extruded aluminium tubes that it is cheaper than the track and travellers. But, for the man who wants to find a quiet anchorage for a meal or for fishing it is a confounded nuisance.

The sail, as it is lowered, comes right out of the groove and must be re-threaded before the sail can be re-set. All of us who like to anchor for quiet periods in odd corners know well that a shift of wind or tide may make it necessary to get under way in a hurry—and here it is that the sail in a groove can be so annoying. To say nothing of that other occasion for wanting to rehoist sail in a hurry: when you are running over a foul tide to a mooring or jetty and find that you have dropped your mainsail too soon and have to get more sail on her again to make your objective. There is, of course, nothing you can do about this without spending more money on the boat. I simply make the point that a good and careful consideration be made of just what it is that you want from your craft before you buy her.

For a boat which is trailed this rig involves the stowing of a spar of anything between 20 and 23 feet in length, and of course the setting up of this long spar into the mast step on arrival at your launching site. The ease with which this is achieved will depend on the help available. Two men can do it easily; a man and a woman will do it with proportionate increase in trouble, while a man on his own may find himself provided with a real tussle.

Fig. 8E, the Gunter Lug. As will be seen from the drawing this rig is very like the Bermudan in its general characteristics—but only superficially so. It has certain very definite advantages over the Bermudan which are worth noting. While it is true that there is a small area of mast where there is both mast and yard the total weight

41

of the wood is no more than in the Bermudan mast because both spars can be a little lighter. When the sail is reefed the gunter yard slides down the mast to lower the centre of gravity of the spars and ease the ship both of weight and windage, and even 5 pounds 20 feet above the deck exerts a leverage of 100 foot-pounds at deck level. It is a point worth remembering when the over-gymnastic crew tries to shin up the mast! He is more likely to turn the boat over than achieve his objective.

I must admit to a great leaning towards a rig which eases the ship as she is reefed and, unlike the Bermudan, the gunter sail is as easily re-hoisted as it is sent down. Again, for those ships which are towed to the water, the mast is very much shorter and it is quite possible to have a rig which approaches the maximum aerodynamic efficiency set on spars all of which stow inside the boat. The advantage of the spars being thus stowed is not only a matter of actual ease of towing on the road. If all will go inside, a cover can protect them all—both spars and boat—and this is a big advantage, as much during the week as when motoring.

Fig. 8G is the Cat Rig. This single-sailed rig was evolved in its present form largely by the Americans. The mast is stepped well forward in the boat and there is no headsail. Its main purpose was to enable a single man to line-fish in a pretty large boat—up to 25 feet in length. There seems to be little point in perpetuating it except in those racing classes intended to be sailed by single-handers.

That finishes the list of rigs needing discussion. We can deal very shortly with the others and only for your interest and the correct classing of the yachts you see as you sail about the creeks and harbours of our coast.

Fig. 8H is a Cutter. That is to say she has two head-sails. There is no other point of difference between a

cutter and a sloop (fig. 8I) which has only one headsail.
In the drawing I have given the cutter a jack-yard topsail
set over a gaff mainsail but she could just as easily have
had a Bermudan mainsail and still be a cutter. The same
applies to a sloop.

Fig. 8J is very modern. She is called a Mast-head Sloop
because in this rig the headsail goes all the way to the
head of the mast and may often be of larger area than the
mainsail. This big sail is not just a light weather sail but
is part of the working canvas of the ship. It may well be
the herald of rigs to come in the future. For it is really
only the physical difficulty of accommodating the mast
aft of its traditional place in the ship which prevents headsails growing bigger and bigger and the boomed mainsail
becoming progressively smaller. And what would we then
have achieved? We'd be pretty well all the way back to
the lateen-shaped loose-footed sails of the Mediterranean
but with a taut wire forestay replacing the heavy lateen
yard, and we'd have a rig with great aerodynamic efficiency
and with enormous lift! The boat in the photograph
facing p. 49 has this sort of rig.

Fig. 8K is a Schooner with the foremast shorter than
the aftermast (now called the main). This and the two
succeeding rigs are entirely big ship rigs where the only
point of dividing the sail plan into patches of smaller area
is to ease the work of handling the sails. Fig. 8L is a
Ketch with the after mast (now known as the mizzen)
forward of the rudder head while fig. 8M is a Yawl which
has a smaller mizzen sail set on a shorter mast which is
stepped abaft the rudder head.

Now we have dealt with the various shapes of sail and
rig we must consider the most suitable cloth of which to
make the sail. In old days flax canvas was the standard
material for yachts going deep-sea, and cotton (of varying

qualities of which Egyptian was the best) was used for the sails of smaller boats. The introduction of synthetic man-made fibre has greatly eased the job of looking after the sails of a yacht, but even so the new Terylene cloths are not foolproof and the man who thinks that all precautions can be dispensed with is in for an expensive shock.

The sails of a yacht are by no means just flat sheets of material sewn together in strips. The whole con-struction is built up in a series of gentle curves by which the draft of a sail is made. It is a fascinating procedure akin to the construction of a hull, and only successful when carried out by experts. In cotton sails the problem of sail-stretch and change of shape in service dictates that the sail be built up of narrow cloths, their direction arranged to suit the flow of the wind over the sail. These cloths are often no more than nine inches from seam-centre to seam-centre. The introduction of synthetic materials with their minimal degree of stretch allows of the " cloths " being greatly increased in width without in-creasing the amount of stretch in the sail. Where a 25-foot leach would previously have had more than 30 cotton cloths, a Terylene sail of the same size would have only seven seams. The great saving in cutting and sewing has meant that, although Terylene is itself a more expensive product than the best cotton, the cost of a synthetic sail when made up is not much more than 15% above that of its cotton counterpart.

Terylene has little capacity to hold water and where a cotton sail in bad weather can add 50% to its weight the Terylene sail gains only 5% of what is, size for size, a much lighter weight. More important still is the relative stability of the new fibres and their resistance to shrinkage and stretch when wet or dried.

Sails of cotton must never be hauled out bar taut on the spars until they have settled. On each of the first six outings they should be stretched a little further and during this stretching period the sail should neither be reefed nor exposed to any great strain. Only when they have been fully stretched should the boat be sailed hard. This is a tedious business not at all suited to our present-day outlook. And again, cotton sails must never be stowed away in a wet or even damp condition or else the mildew spots will soon speckle their virgin whiteness. If sails are wet the lashings must be eased up as soon as the boat enters harbour and the sails hung out to dry at the first opportunity.

Nevertheless, synthetic fibres have problems of their own. In a cotton sail the stitches of the seam are drawn tight and sink into the cloth, obtaining from it a great deal of protection against chafe—that arch-enemy of the seaman. But in a Terylene sail the cloth is so resistant to compression that the sewing thread lies above the seam, waiting to be worn away against the shrouds. And, though it is true that Terylene cannot support mildew by itself, it must be remembered that mildew is a fungus which can grow quite effectively in the dust which collects in the interstices of any cloth. Furthermore both it and its spores exude a stain which will attack synthetic yarn. The long and the short of it is that, unless precautions are taken, the effect is much the same as in the case of a cotton sail.

Terylene sails should be thoroughly washed at the end of the season before being put away for the winter, and, if their drying takes only minutes instead of hours, they still need attention before being put away even for so short a period as a week.

The action of the wind on the sails of a boat is interesting and supremely important for the seaman, and as it is his prime method of progress he should understand the basic reason why a boat sails at all, because in acquiring this knowledge he will more easily determine how to trim his own sails when he gets afloat.

The function of the bowed shape of a sail is not entirely analogous to that of an aeroplane's wing. The design of the latter is concerned primarily with lift over drag, and it has an engine to pull or push it forward thus creating its own wind over the surface, whereas the boat has no engine and must rely on what the Good Lord sends in the way of weather. Again, whereas the aeroplane wing is a rigid aerofoil concerned with high wind speeds, the sail is a flexible one dealing only with relatively low speeds. A sail made from a heavy cloth, because it retains its shape, may have less heeling effort and less drag than a lighter cloth, while the greater relative forward drive will allow the boat to sail more nearly upright and, because the hull form will be better the nearer she is to the vertical, she will go faster through the water.

To understand the shape that a sail should be we must realise that the wind flows separately down each side of the sail. The flow on the leeward side is stronger than that on the weather side, because, owing to the sail's curvature, the wind must go a longer distance round the lee side of the curve before it meets again at the leach. This faster flowing air causes a reduction of pressure on the lee side while the slower air on the weather side builds up pressure. The pressure differential can be expressed as a series of arrows perpendicular to the sail surface at various places on the curve, the length of the arrow denoting the relative force. See fig. 11.

From fig. 11 we can learn two lessons. It will be realised that the total driving force could be expressed as a single vector whose length would be the sum of all the small arrows and the direction would be the weighted average of them all. So long as this single arrow points forward of the beam, the ship moves forward; if it is aft of the beam

46

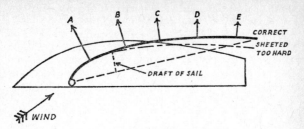

Fig. 11

the ship stops and begins to gather sternway, while if it is dead on the beam the ship will merely heel over. As the apparent wind will move forward and away from the beam as the ship's speed is increased we can see why, if a boat is allowed to lose speed (say when a helmsman bungles his tack) she will heel fiercely as soon as the sails do fill to the wind of the new tack, simply because she is not travelling fast enough through the water. For this reason the experienced helmsman puts his helm down slowly when he goes about and uses only just enough rudder to achieve his purpose because he realises, even if he does not know the reason for it, that his speed must be maintained if he is not to be heeled over by the wind—which in turn would imply a further loss of speed.

The second lesson which we have from fig. 11 is given us by the line drawn in dots and dashes and marked at its end with the words " sheeted too hard." If this line is compared with the correct set of the sail it will be seen that although arrow B might be slightly longer it would (being perpendicular to the sail surface) be pointed more nearly towards the beam while the arrows C, D and E will all be of greater force. In thus sheeting sail too close to

47

the wind we have greatly increased the heeling force and now the single vector, the average of all the arrows, will be pointing nearer the beam. If I were asked what was the most common fault of the novice I would answer without hesitation " sheeting his sails too close, with the mistaken idea that a boat can be made to go to windward simply by hardening the sheets until he has taken all the ' lift ' and the drive from the sail."

It must be pointed out that the arrows A and B in fig. 11 are not likely to be so large if only the mainsail is used. They were drawn on the assumption that a jib was set. The function of a headsail is supremely important. It increases the speed of the wind flow on the lee side of the sail by what is known as the Venturi effect. This, without being too technical, is the same effect that a fireman gets from the nozzle of his hose: a fluid passing down a pipe with a gradual reduction of bore increases its velocity as it leaves the narrower opening, and in this case wind acts as if it were a fluid. Before we go on to have a look at how this works and what effect the correct or incorrect sheeting of the headsails may have, it is worth pointing out that from the first three sentences of this paragraph we have the reason why, if we are caught out by a sudden increase in the strength of the wind, taking in the jib will at once ease the situation. The boat is then not only relieved of the area of the headsail but the heeling and driving forces of the mainsail are reduced.

Fig. 12 is devoted entirely to headsails. Diagram A shows the jib correctly set with the Venturi effect functioning to perfection. But in diagram B we have a headsail sheeted too hard (or where the sheet lead is too far inboard). It will be seen that this will not only destroy the principle of the gradual reduction in the flow but will direct wind into the luff of the mainsail and cause it to belly inwards towards the centre-line of the ship. Diagram

The "Yachting Monthly" *Senior*. A very attractive 16-foot two-berth sloop designed by Kenneth M. Gibbs. (*Photo. Yachting Monthly.*)

The author's *Orchid*, 24 feet in length and weighing 32 cwt., with three berths. This is about the limit of easy trailing.

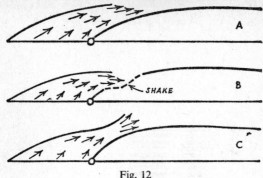

Fig. 12

C shows the effect that may be expected from a jib with a slack leach. It is to avoid this that the better jibs are fitted with a leach-line in the seam which enables the tension on this part of the sail to be varied.

Reverting to fig. 11 we can see the reason for, and the great benefit obtained by, the use of battens in the leach of the mainsail. For, if the after end of the mainsail is allowed to fall into a curve, it will be obvious that the little arrows D and E will point even more backwards. We can also see from this figure that with a loose-footed sail without a boom it will be very difficult indeed for the novice to sheet his sail too hard: and that a boom being by nature a straight spar has the habit of destroying the draft of a sail for two or three feet above it unless the sail in question has been very expertly cut.

There could be a point made for one or two battens in the leach of the headsail in the case of fig. 12. The effect described in this diagram is generally shown by a continual fluttering of the leach and is most liable to occur in the case of narrow headsails. The storm jib of my own yacht, designed to reduce heeling movement to a minimum and to be no more than a " slot " to the mainsail, was made very high and narrow—and at first suffered from this defect until I had three small nine-inch battens set in the leach, which quite cured the trouble.

I hope then, that I have shown in this chapter that there is a deal of knowledge concerned with making a success of going to sea: knowledge which is almost as much fun to collect as it is to use.

CHAPTER 5

No boat is ever big enough to take in safety all the people who may sometimes want to go in her—A limit to the capacity must be fixed—Suggested limits—A boat can greatly reduce the cost of the annual holiday—But she should be able to be rowed, sailed or motored with equal facility—The size of the outboard must match the size of the boat—Suggested engine power for various sizes of craft—Time necessary to service boats of various constructions—Must be related to the time the owner can devote to the work—The small trailerable cruiser: goes up in size by the cube not by the linear measurement—With her more than ever the sail must be able to be taken down and re-set with ease.

By this time the reader should have come to some sort of decision as to the type of craft best suited to his temperament, his pocket, the time he can spare for maintenance, the rig he prefers and, perhaps most important, the number of people he is going to take along with him.

I have purposely cast the last sentence of the preceeding paragraph in this rather protesting form because it is a sad fact that there has never yet been a boat big enough to accommodate all the people who, from time to time, will try to go sailing with you. The plain fact is that every boat has its limit to which the wise owner will most rigidly adhere. And the more nearly he approaches the state of being a complete novice the more adamant he should be. Even for the most experienced owner, extra people in the boat always make sailing difficult. To handle a boat one needs a certain minimum of space wherein to move and this does not diminish with the size of the craft. It is a constant feature. Similarly, your crew will need a given space in which they may rise, twist their bodies, pause as the ship passes through the wind's eye and then

51

re-position themselves on the new weather side. Any interruption of this manœuvre by the clash of bodies is dangerous.

The first thing then is to decide the number of people, which will in turn decide the minimum overall size. The number of people that can sail will be about half the number which the same boat can carry when under oars or outboard motor, and so we come to what is probably, for sailing, a reasonable answer: that for four people the boat should be 14 feet long, for two people 9 to 11 feet, and that boats below this length can only be sailed in comfort and safety by a single person. These simple equations have taken no regard for age and size which may seem a trifle unfair. It is probable that if these numbers were taken as being those for grown-up people it would be reasonable to substitute two children for one adult in arriving at the total compliment. But I do think that this should be done only once. That is to say that the fourteen-foot boat might be asked to sail with either four adults or with three adults and two children under fifteen. She should not be asked to carry two grown-ups and four children. For the latter crew a sixteen-foot boat would be needed.

I think that the matching of the boat's size to the probable crew is most important because it may well be decisive in answering the next question—the question of how much money should be spent on the first cost of the boat and her gear. And here I would introduce a point which has been most noticeable in my own life. A boat of your own does reduce the cost of the annual holiday. It provides a constant source of pleasure and, even on wet days, an occupation in servicing her and looking after her gear. This is a saving in one expense which I am sure can validly and with profit be put towards another in the family budget and could well be the deciding factor as to whether to buy a boat at all.

If this is true, and I believe it is so, then the boat you buy should be a versatile creature, equally at home under oars, outboard motor or sail. For there will, in the course of the normal holiday be times when she will be required to function under any one of these three methods of propulsion. The opinion is often expressed that a good sailing boat cannot be expected to handle well under motor and that a motor-boat cannot be expected to sail. Now this is true only when the planing hull of a fast hydroplane is compared with the planing hull of the out-and-out sailing machine. The normal hull of the type we have discussed in chapter 3 should be (provided it is a good design) an adequate performer under any means of propulsion.

The point to bear in mind is that a good sailing hull will take an outboard motor with complete satisfaction to the owner so long as the engine power is not too great. And so we come to another table of constants. A well-designed sailing hull of 14 feet will take an outboard engine of up to 10 horse power. That is the limit. A six or seven horse power engine would probably suit her equally well and give almost the same performance at a greatly reduced expenditure. Speed, beyond the natural speed of a hull (approximately the square root of the waterline length multiplied by $1\frac{1}{3}$) is very expensive of fuel. A 12-foot boat will take a motor from four to six horse power and a 10-foot boat will get along very nicely with a three horse power engine. For boats below 10 feet in length a motor of one and a half horse power is adequate, while very small boats in the seven- and eight-foot range should only have engines of minimal horse power.

We have dealt with the physical properties of the various building materials and so there is only left for comment the question of the time which the buyer has available for servicing his own boat—unless, of course, he proposes to have this done for him by some local painter. The fact remains that a wooden boat needs re-painting each season, and there is quite a lot of work in this. If she is varnished she must be sandpapered right down until the surface is smooth all over and all the places where the varnish surface has been chipped are no longer sharp edged. She will then need two coats of varnish with a good rubbing down with wet-and-dry 320 paper between coats. If she is painted, the dents in the surface must first be filled with a marine stopper which is wet-flatted smooth and then the whole hull rubbed down and given a coat of flatting and one or two coats of enamel with again a rub down between each coat. (For the last rub down before the final coat of enamel I prefer 400 grain paper.) All this takes time and there will be the mast and spars to be varnished as well. In fact the doing of all this is as likely as not to take up just as many hours in the winter as you have sailed in the summer.

Now this is all right if you have the time and you like doing the work, for it turns boat owning into an all-the-year-round hobby, but if you are not prepared to mortgage this amount of your life and you cannot afford a painter's bill, you would be well advised to consider fibre-glass. Then all that is necessary is to rub down the scratches with a fine graded nitro-cellulose polishing compound and go over the whole exterior with the same hard wax polish that is used with motor cars. Most people prefer to have some woodwork on their fibre-glass boats and there are some technical reasons why certain parts—the gunwales and seats for example—are better made of African mahogany or Parana pine. But these pieces which are usually varnished are few in number and very small in area compared with the total surface of a wooden boat. One week-end's work, Saturday and Sunday, should be sufficient to do all that is necessary of winter maintenance before the summer's sailing.

There is one sort of boat which had best be dealt with shortly in this chapter: I refer to the small sailing cruiser which can be trailed with almost the same facility as the open sailing boat. But first a word of warning. Boats get enormously bigger as they go up in size—much more so than the usual comparison of one dimension alone, i.e. length, will suggest. Their size goes up by the cube. The cube of a boat 14 feet long, 4 feet in beam, and 2 feet deep is 112; that of a boat 18 feet by 5 by $2\frac{1}{2}$ is 225. This difference truly represents the increase in size from the smaller to the larger craft. An 18-foot boat is *twice* as big as one of 14 feet.

The definition of a " small trailerable cruiser " goes all the way from " dinghies with lids on " to craft which are fit, within reason, to go anywhere. At the moment I am living aboard my own boat (which is trailed home at the end of each season) for the purpose of writing this book and I am living in very considerable comfort. I have very nearly six feet of headroom, three berths, a gas stove, inboard engine and all the bits and pieces to make life afloat both comfortable and safe.

The purchase of this sort of boat must be approached with great care and with even more thought of exactly what it is that you want from your new purchase. To begin with, the fitting of a cabin takes much room and, when the ship is sailing, it forces the movable weight of the crew towards the small cockpit in the stern—a cockpit which is even more subject to overcrowding than the whole length of an open boat. In fact, although my own ship is 24 feet in length and weighs 32 hundredweights, we find that three is the maximum number we can accommodate and really she is best with two—except during a passage, when one of the three will probably be found in a bunk!

In the smaller sizes these " small sailing cruisers " can

carry no more than two people in comfort and, although in the dealer's showroom they may look big enough to go anywhere, to live aboard one for even a night is like living under the kitchen table. Now there is absolutely nothing wrong in this. A great deal of fun can be had in these little boats. You can sleep where you fetch up, and there is always blessed shelter from the rigours of an English summer within their tiny cabins. All I ask is that you realise what you are in for and remember all the time that the smaller ones are, as I have said, no more than dinghies with lids on. They should never be taken on passages which could not be undertaken by an open boat of the same waterline length. To treat the smaller ones as if they were fully fledged yachts is to court disaster. If this is borne in mind, and if there are only two of you in a 16-foot boat or three in a 20-foot boat, they can give an enormous amount of fun and will save your holiday hotel bills. I have no compunction in again mentioning the question of cost in a context where it is even more pertinent than with the day-sailer.

As far as sailing these cruisers is concerned, the advice in this book is just as suitable for a boat with a cabin as it is for one that is only an open boat, although I would very seriously refer the intending purchaser of this sort of craft to the remarks in chapter 4 on the disadvantages of having a mainsail where the luff runs in a groove up the mast. In a small cabin boat it is much more difficult (because one cannot hoist the sail without standing on deck) to get under way in a hurry when the mainsail goes up in a groove. I do feel most strongly that any arrangement other than the one which permits the sail to lower and yet remain secure to the mast and ready to re-hoist is most unseamanlike and most dangerous.

CHAPTER 6

What gear and spares to carry—The parts of an anchor—Types of anchor compared—The cable and warp—The amount of cable to lay out—The contents of the boat bag—Buoyancy bags for the boat—Personal buoyancy for the crew and especially for children.

Once the question of whether to buy a boat or not has been decided, and when you know the type of boat you are looking for, there comes the problem of what gear she will need. In this, personal preference will again be the deciding factor and the amount of extra gear will vary enormously from those over-careful owners who feel they must carry every conceivable spare with them to those foolhardy gentlemen who are quite happy to launch their craft on to the waters with no gear beyond that which the boat had when she was in the showroom.

To my mind both extremes are wrong. The boats under discussion are day-sailers and not cruisers, and they will seldom be away from their base (whether it be a trailer or a club compound) for more than a few hours. To overload a boat with gear beyond that which can be given safe and waterproof stowage seems to me to be pointless and, because there is nothing worse than loose ends of gear lying about, dangerous.

So let us compile a list of gear required for a 14-foot day boat, either sail or motor. The first thing to buy will be an anchor and some method of connecting it to the boat.

Anchors are of various kinds and will repay a little study. The traditional, or Fisherman, anchor is a fellow

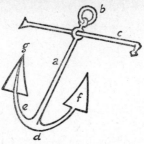

Fig. 13

of many parts, having a shank (a), ring (b), stock (c), crown (d), arms (e), flukes (f) and a bill (g). See fig. 13.

If weight were of no consideration these anchors in deep water and good holding ground would be hard to beat. In comparison with other types, however, they have to be almost twice the weight to give the same degree of holding power and they have the great disadvantage that when doing their work one arm is in the sea bed and the other sticking up at right angles, just waiting to pierce the boat's bottom should the falling tide leave her dry and she decide to sit upon her own anchor. And again, if she should be carried round her anchor by wind or tide she will drag a loop of the cable round the upstanding arm and at once be riding to foul anchor—traditionally the negation of safety.

Cruisers, having two such anchors and in danger of being swung round their cable, would not take this risk. They would lay out two anchors and ride between them— a process known as mooring. It would seem, then, that for our boat which will have but a single anchor one of the other types should be chosen. They fall into two classes,

58

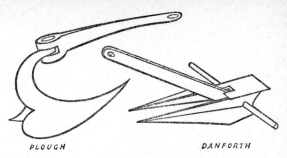

PLOUGH   DANFORTH

Fig. 14

those that have a tool resembling a ploughshare (or perhaps a better description would be a potato ridger) at the end of a shank and those which are like small editions of a big ship's anchor but have the stock welded across the base of wide flukes. The latter are generally known as Danforths. Fig. 14.

Here again the holding power of the Ploughshare anchor is less, weight for weight, than that of the other, but as both will be much lighter than the Fisherman this is not very important. Our boat would be considered to have adequate ground tackle if she had a seven-pound Danforth, a 10-pound Ploughshare, or a 20-pound Fisherman, and I do not know which of the first two I would choose. Three seasons ago I bought for my own cruiser one of each to try to decide which was the better. The only comment I have is that the ploughshare can nip your fingers as the share swings about its pivot and that the Danforth can go down foul if it is let go in a hurry and the chain jams between the swivelling shank and the fluke. As neither of these two criticisms seems worth very much, the answer is

59

still unproved. On the other hand I have the distinct impression that the Danforth is the better in soft mud while the Ploughshare has the advantage in sand or rock.

For our boat, then, we will choose the Danforth because it is not only the lightest but it stows slightly closer than the Plough. What really matters is with what we choose to connect the anchor to the ship, and in this I am quite prepared to be dogmatic. Some chain—at least four fathoms of 3/16 in.—is necessary to act as a " spring " between the anchor ring and the warp. It is neither a question of strength nor of possible chafe against rocks on the bed of the sea. It is made necessary by the importance of providing a weight to keep the pull on the anchor parallel to the bottom of the sea and to help prevent the boat " snubbing " at her anchor.

For a warp we shall need some 15 to 20 fathoms of $1\frac{1}{2}$ in. rope, depending on the depths in the waters in which we are to sail. But as this may make rather a large and troublesome coil in a small boat it might be as well if we cut it and keep it in two halves. There will be plenty of occasions when we shall need to use only the one piece. Ropes of synthetic fibre—being so much stronger than those of the traditional materials, hemp or sisal—can be that much thinner. But here a word of warning—there is a minimum limit to the size of rope that can be comfortably gripped by the hand, and to reduce the anchor warp to the thinner rope by opting for Terylene or nylon could be to end up with a line so thin that it cannot be hauled upon. And in this connection it must be remembered that we have already decided that gear should be kept to a minimum and that our anchor warps will be asked to double their duty with that of the mooring lines and the towing hawser.

In text books on the sea you will generally find it stated that a ship should be brought to her anchor with enough

cable out to be the equal of three times the depth of
water when the tide is high (and don't forget the tide!).
But this advice is, I think, for big ships which are very
unlikely to bring up in places where the waves will be
large enough to throw them back on their anchors.
They will have only the wind and the tide with which to
compete. A small boat frequently has to anchor in waves
which are relatively much greater and so I personally
always give my little ship five times the depth of water.

What more in the way of gear? You'll need first a
" boat bag " containing a spare of each size of shackle
aboard, a hank of codline and a small ball of tarred
marline. You'll also need a baler of some sort, or a pump,
preferably both.

Then of gear which could more properly be described
as boat fittings there is, unless buoyancy has been built
into the hull, the question of providing enough bags to
support the boat and her crew in the case of a capsize or
of serious damage. To omit this is suicidal, for we have to
realise that sailing can never be an entirely safe sport—
nor would we wish that it should be so else the thrill would
be gone and the personal triumph over the wind and tide
be made void. This is to encourage preparedness and to
discourage foolhardiness. To overlook the question of
buoyancy for the boat is to be as foolhardy as to go to sea
without personal buoyancy for everyone aboard. Points
to remember in deciding how much to carry are that it
should be stowed as high as possible in the boat and
securely fastened, otherwise it may either come out or else
(if it is low in the boat) will cause her to prefer to float
bottom-up and be very difficult to right after a capsize. In
the case of a wooden boat she will, when filled, have
positive or only very slight negative buoyancy and so not
much more need be given her beyond that which will carry
the weight of the crew in water. But a fibre-glass boat will

remain a dead weight all the time, and with her enough must be carried to support her own weight as well as that of the crew.

We are back now to a factor governing the first choice of your boat, particularly if you have developed a leaning towards one of fibre-glass construction. With this material the tanks are nearly always " built in " and it is most important to see that the boat you buy has tanks which come nearly, if not quite, up to the level of the gunwale.

Every big steamship carries lifebelts or personal buoyancy for all her passengers and crew. How very much more particular the small ship should be to see that everyone she takes to sea has his own lifebelt or life-saving jacket. And yet how many go to sea without this elementary precaution or, worse still, have them aboard and are found not to have been wearing them when disaster arrived. In one week-end last year no less than four lives were lost in one south coast area from this one error alone. Every year reports are received of boats found crewless and drifting, the inference being that someone has fallen overboard and the other, in trying to get him aboard, has gone too. If the first man had been wearing a jacket the whole delicate business of recovering him from the water could have been dealt with more slowly and with much greater certainty.

There are many good smocks on the market. Some (from the legacy of wartime procedure) inflate by releasing compressed air from a small cylinder, others (to be preferred because they need no such conscious triggering by the wearer) contain within their double folds enough trapped air to support a man, and by the construction of the panels of which they are made they ensure that the wearer shall float face upwards.

Children should always wear jackets. At one time a question of the personal pride of the immature might have made them unwilling to don life-saving gear, but now that all racing boats are manned by jacketed crews there should be no difficulty in persuading the children to emulate their elders. If racing men sailing known courses within sight of the club-house or committee boat think it worth while to wear jackets, surely the day sailor, alone on the seas and far from help from his fellows, should do so too.

CHAPTER 7

The seamanlike knot is as readily untied as it is made—The clove hitch on an open bar—The bowline—The clove hitch on a closed bar—The round turn and two half hitches—The bow hitch—The sheet bend—The double sheet bend—The sheet bend with ends stopped—The overhand knot and the figure of eight—The eye splice—The back splice—The sailmaker's whipping—Methods of securing the ends of synthetic fibre ropes.

Before we can go afloat and discuss the matter of sailing we must make sure that we can tie a seamanlike knot. It is surprising that a civilisation which can dispatch men into space and return them alive has not yet taught all its members to tie the simpler knots. If you don't believe me, try to undo the string that surrounds the average parcel! Indeed this matter of parcels is worth close investigation. There you will see the same inefficient knot repeated over and over again in the quaint belief that repetition alone is enough to obtain security. Whereas the truth is that one knot correctly made would have both made the parcel secure and allowed it to be undone by the recipient.

The analogy is complete. It is as important that a knot can be unfastened as that it be fastened at all. Life at sea would be altogether too expensive if the knife was the only means of undoing the wrongly-tied rope; and yet one frequently recognises the body in rain-lashed oilskins that is bent over some knot while its fingers, probably with torn and bleeding nails, attempt unavailingly to cast loose the rain-shrunk coils of the improperly tied rope. The speed of release can be even more important than the speed of tying up. I well remember, when I was a very new midshipman, the coxwain of the old *Tiger's* first picket

boat saying to me as he cast off the last and utterly re-
dundant hitch of a line I had just made fast, " I see you're
one of these three hitch men, sir." The " sir," of course,
was pure naval usage and courtesy for he was a better seaman than I will ever be, but he had made his point and went
on to enlarge on it by pointing out that " a round turn
and two half hitches " would hold more than the rope
would take and that a third hitch would only delay our
getting away.

I have never forgotten this lesson learnt on a night of
full gale with the picket boat cavorting madly alongside
the jetty where we had gone to collect the ship's captain.

The knots which you will need are really very few and
simple and, as each has its uses, we can take it from that
aspect and deal first with the matter of tying the boat up.
Now there are really only two alternative fixtures to which
a boat is made fast, the first is a post, such as a bollard,
the top of which is " open," the second is a bar which is
" closed," as in the hand rail of a pier. A ring is, of course,
only a closed bar bent round in a circle!

Dealing first with the open post we have the clove
hitch as the best method of securing a rope tightly to an
upright stump. To make this, two loops are thrown as in
fig. 15 and these are then dropped over the post and pulled
tight.

By taking both free ends and pushing them together,
a clove hitch can always be slackened off. Its advantages
are that it does leave one end free for some other purpose,
and that it can be made anywhere along the rope without
even having a free end at all.

There will be occasions, however, when going through
locks or alongside piers where the level is always above
that of the ship, when a loop in the end of a rope will be
preferable. A bowline will be the easiest method of making
the loop.

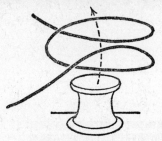

CLOVE HITCH ON AN OPEN POST

Fig. 15

To make a bowline first make a loop in the rope with that part which leads to the end of the rope uppermost as you hold it before you (A in fig. 16). The rope-end is brought up through this loop and passed round behind the standing part, B, to finish down through the loop as C.

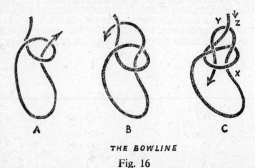

THE BOWLINE

Fig. 16

The bowline, if subjected to strain and wet, can be difficult to undo unless you know the trick. To loosen the knot of a bowline hold the part of the loop and the end of the rope firmly in the fingers of the left hand where marked X in fig. 16C. The grip should be as close to the knot as possible. Then with the fingers of the right hand draw and work the top of the loop at Y towards you, alternating your work with downward pushes at Z.

We must now go back and consider tying up to the closed bar. Here again the clove hitch can be used but now the method of working it is different.

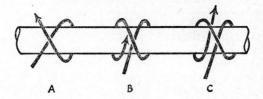

THE CLOVE HITCH ON A CLOSED BAR

Fig. 17

The rope is first thrown over the top of the bar and brought up over itself, pointing towards the left. Fig. 17A. It is then passed round again (B) and lastly brought up under itself to finish as at C.

The clove hitch is a useful one for ties which are of short duration where a firm grip is needed, and the ease of letting go is important. It suffers from a tendency to loosen itself if the working part is short and the rope stiff and wet; then the bobbing of a boat tied short to the ring of a catamaran can loosen the hitch. When tying up for a longer period of time to either the " open " post or

" closed " bar the best is the clumsily named round-turn-and-two-half-hitches. In this the rope completely circles the spar and then makes a clove hitch on the standing part. (See fig. 18).

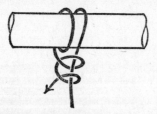

ROUND-TURN-AND-TWO-HALF-HITCHES

Fig. 18

This is a hitch which does not jam and which can be relied upon to hold for as long as the rope does not chafe itself through on rough ironwork. With this hitch we could leave the tying up business if it related only to the boats themselves and did not also cover the hundred and one other little tying jobs which crop up such as securing the lacing of the boat cover, of rowlock lashings to the boat, and of any rope to an eye plate or screw eye. There is no fury like that of a man delayed because the line he wishes to cast off is too valuable to cut and rain or spray has made its easing impossible. And for this there is a most valuable hitch for which I have never been able to discover the correct name nor have I ever seen it described in any seamanship manual. I call it the bow hitch which seems a good enough name, and have illustrated it in fig. 19.

To make this hitch you pass the rope's end through the eye away from you and towards the right, drawing all the end through the eye; then bring the rope end round

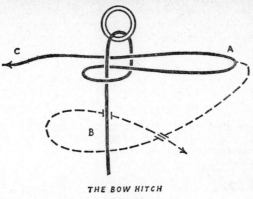

THE BOW HITCH
Fig. 19

over the standing part of the rope and double it to make a big loop (A). This loop is next drawn through the first turn to make a half hitch, and lastly the loop is used to take another hitch round the standing part as at B. This is a hitch which will never jam no matter how thin the line with which it is made. All the strain is taken by the first hitch which can always be undone by a sharp pull on the end (C). The second hitch (B) is no more than a preventer to stop an inadvertent pull from slipping the hitch.

Every picture tells a story, even when it is a warning. On the dinghy landing stage which I can see if I look through my scuttle there are already, this early in the season, four short and cut lengths of dinghy painter, and in each case the other end of the rope is secured to the staging by a novel and quite unfastenable knot. I am willing to bet that in each case the history is the same. The party came ashore to dine (or merely to wine) at the hotel that stands by the little pier. Then, when the time came to return, the water had risen sufficiently to wet the improper knot. Coming back, perhaps in the rain, the owners cut the rope they could not cast off. One wonders how many more lengths will hang from the stage when autumn comes!

So much for tying up. We must now discuss the other main purpose for which a knot is used at sea—the joining together of two ropes, or the ends of the same rope. In this respect the landsman's impression of the sailor is that he is a man who never ties a " granny." Which is all right as far as it goes, but then, except for the purpose suggested by its name, a sailor rarely ties a reef knot either! The fact is that this knot will only hold when the rope with which it is made passes round something which is as solid as a spar, or as semi-solid as a roll of sailcloth. Out in the open on its own, and used to join two ropes together, it can come undone as easily as a granny, and perhaps more easily, for all that is required to undo it is to take hold of the two parts and push them smartly together.

The correct method of joining two ropes together is to use the sheet bend. And here it might be as well to consider the seaman's exact use of the words knot, hitch and bend, because, when we understand the significance he attaches to them, we shall have gone a long way towards learning which to use when, and why. The knot is for parcelling something up, the hitch is for securing one object to another by a single line which allows of some independent movement between the objects, and the bend is for joining two ropes together. For this purpose the sheet bend, fig. 20, is most usually employed.

To make a sheet bend, double back the end of one rope to form a loop and hold this in your left hand, then pass the end of the other rope up through this loop towards you as in fig. 20A. Next take this end down outside the

70

THE SHEET BEND

Fig. 20

loop and round the other side as in B. Lastly dip the end under the bridge formed by the second rope's passage through the loop to make the complete bend (C). This bend can always be easily undone by pushing down on the end of the loop.

There is an impression about that this bend is meant to be used only when the ropes to be joined are of unequal thickness. I can only assume that this belief has grown up because, when ropes of dissimilar size and type are in use, the reef knot is particularly unreliable as a method of effecting a join. The sheet bend is just as useful and reliable whatever the size of the ropes may be, and the only point to remember is that when joining ropes of different size, it is the thicker one which should be formed into the loop and the thinner one which should be worked round it.

If the ropes are of very different size—say a heaving

71

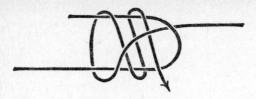

THE DOUBLE SHEET BEND
Fig. 21

line bent on to a hawser—the lighter rope can be passed
round twice to form a double sheet bend, fig. 21. And
this double bend can be used too (even when they are of
the same size) if the ropes are slippery with weed or have
been contaminated with fuel oil.

If the ropes used are of similar size, I find that the double
bend can often be difficult to undo, and if I do not trust the
surface of the ropes I prefer to stop the two loose ends to
their standing parts with a length of tarred marline, as
illustrated in fig. 22.

THE SHEET BEND WITH ENDS "STOPPED"
Fig. 22

This bend is, of course, equally useful for securing the free end of a rope to some pre-formed loop—such as an eye which has already been spliced in the end of another rope. If the eye is " soft " and the ropes are of approximately the same size, the single bend can be used. But if the eye is " hard " and contains a metal thimble it is best to use the double bend which will not then be so inclined to jam, because the friction of the metal will be much less than if the eye had been all rope.

With the sheet bend mastered we can complete the list of essential bends and hitches in which proficiency should be achieved before any man, woman or child is allowed to take a boat afloat, and there now remains only one final piece of ropework to be dealt with—the figure of eight.

When a rope such as a main or jib sheet passes through a fairlead or eye plate there will be a need to prevent its end from being inadvertently pulled through the lead. To stop this happening one only too frequently sees an overhand knot tied in the end of the rope—A in fig. 23.

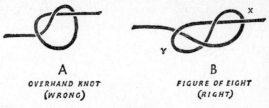

A
OVERHAND KNOT
(WRONG)

B
FIGURE OF EIGHT
(RIGHT)

Fig. 23

This is an extremely dangerous knot because if the rope should ever run out until the knot has to do its job it will be pulled so tight that it will be impossible to undo, and there are few places where delay in casting off a knot could be more dangerous. The proper knot to use is the figure of eight, fig. 23B. It is made by forming the rope-end into a loop with the short end lying over and above the standing part of the rope. This end is then passed underneath the rope, brought up and back and then pushed down through the loop. This knot will never jam and can easily be released by pressing downwards at X and Y at the same time.

To take even a glance at ropework is to venture into a sea so vast that no single man knows, or ever knew, all the intricacies of the art. It must be remembered that of the many methods of working the sennits and stoppers of various kinds, only a few were ever put to practical use. This work was one of the ways of passing the time in the age of sail and examples of the finished decoration, no longer seen in even the most fusty of shore-side junk shops, have passed for ever from the world of ships. For our purpose we are left with only two that we need to know, the eye splice and the back splice.

In the eye splice, fig. 24, the rope is first unlayed for a distance equivalent to five times the circumference of the rope. The end of the rope is then bent into a loop, having first separated the three strands, leaving the middle strand (1) on top of the rope. This middle and separated strand is then tucked under the top strand of the rope from right to left (A).

Next the separated strand which lies on your left of the centre one (2) is forced under the next strand of rope to the left of the first tuck. If the rope does not open easily, a way under it can be forced with a round marline spike before this second tuck is attempted (B).

Then comes the only tricky part. The last separated strand (3) is led back towards the right at the same time that the work is turned round to the left until the strand of rope not already used comes uppermost (C). Then

74

tuck the separated strand (3) under this one *still passing it from right to left*. This, until it is pulled tight, may appear to be an awkward tuck but you will soon get the hang of it. You will now have the separated strands each standing out between one of the lays of the rope.

Still working from right to left, each strand in turn is given another tuck, passing over one rope strand and under the next. On completion of the second tuck the strands will be standing out again regularly between each lay. Next make the third tuck. Then rub the splice well between the hands or under the ball of the foot against the deck depending on the size of rope being worked, and cut off the ends, leaving a little spare to prevent the natural working of the rope allowing the strands to escape.

If you wish to make a particularly " tiddly " job you

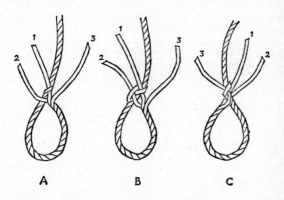

THE EYE SPLICE
Fig. 24

may serve over the cut off ends. Otherwise, for ordinary use, I should leave it as it is.

The other splice, the back splice, is a very useful way of finishing off the end of a warp to prevent its unravelling. It must be admitted however that to do this does double the circumference of the rope over the splice, and therefore it is not suitable where the rope has to be passed through a small hole or sheave. But for the rough work of a mooring warp or hawser I prefer it to the more usual whipping, which can so frequently come off just when you have least time in which to replace it before a great deal of the rope has unlayed itself and gone to waste.

To back-splice a rope first unlay the rope as we did for the eye splice, but allow a little more to be unlayed, about six times the circumference of the rope. Then hold the rope upwards with the unlayed strands falling down and outward like the petals of a more than mature flower. Turn the rope slowly in the fingers until an open V of the lay is towards you and one particular strand (which we will call number 1, or the " master " strand) lies directly beyond the V. See fig. 25. It is easier to draw than explain. Take this master strand and bring it up and towards you to make a loop. Then take the strand on

THE CROWN – THE FIRST PART OF A BACK SPLICE

Fig. 25

your left (2) over the end of the first loop *and behind* the untouched strand on the right. Lastly take the strand on your right (3) and dip it through the first loop. Then work the knot into shape.

You have now made a crown knot and are ready to look at the work from the other end, when you will see that, as in the eye splice, each unlayed strand has its own rope strand to be tucked under, working from right to left over one and under one. Make three tucks and then rub or roll out the work and cut off the ends.

A very important skill to acquire is the making of a satisfactory whipping. One method frequently taught is to pull the ends back under the turns with a loop, but, if the turns are as tight as they should be, I can never induce the loop to pull the end back! If it does do so, I know that the whipping will soon come off. The best whipping of all for a yachtsman's use is that called the "sailmaker's." It is not easy to explain, but I will try. If you cannot understand it I do suggest you find someone who can teach you the simple trick. The knowledge is very well worth acquiring.

This whipping will stand harder wear than any other. Traditionally it was used for reef points, awning stops and for any other small rope exposed to the wind. First unlay the rope for about three circumferences. Separate the strands and hold the rope as for making a crown knot but with the strands standing up (being shorter than for a splice they should co-operate in this). Take about twenty-four inches of twine and make a loop about eight inches long in one end. Pass this loop over the No. 1, or "master" strand with the two ends towards you and lying in the V between strands 2 and 3. Hold with the left hand the loop of the twine some inches down the back of the rope and the two loose ends of twine down the front. With the right hand lay up the rope again, and then, taking the long end of twine, wind it round the freshly layed up rope against the lay. Work towards the end of the rope until sufficient turns have been put on. I find this whipping so efficient that, in comparison with others, far less turns will suffice. I use six full turns for ordinary work, eight turns where the work will be exceptionally severe.

Now pull up the original loop outside the work, following the lay of the master strand, and pass it over that strand where it comes out above the turns of the serving twine. Then haul on the short end to draw the loop tight. This will be found to run quite easily, and when it is tight the loop will be found to have nipped the serving turns so that they cannot come loose.

You now have the two ends of the serving twine to settle. One is sprouting out from below the serving, the other is nipped above. You take the lower one and, following up the lay of the rope, you tie it (with a reef knot) to the other end in the middle of the rope, where it will be protected by the unlayed ends.

Lastly you cut off the ends rather farther from the top of the serving twine than with the normal whipping and tease out the ends of the rope to hide the reef knot.

So far, in the splices and whippings which we have considered, we have assumed that the rope was of the traditional materials, sisal, hemp, manilla or coir. The new man-made materials present special problems of their own because, as soon as the lay is touched, they immediately unravel far beyond the point intended unless precautions have been taken. When working ropes of Terylene or nylon it is necessary to prevent their unlaying by the application of bands of adhesive cellophane strip such as is used for parcels and to cut these away when the work is completed. But, if they are more troublesome in this way than the older materials they do have the advantage that they are thermo-plastic and so the ends may be heat-bonded together over a flame. When so softened the resultant mass can be moulded into shape by well-licked fingers. In fact this can be so effective that, in the smaller sizes, such as leach lines, batten ties, and for ropes up to codline size, whippings may be dispensed with altogether and the heat-bonded seal be made quite effective enough for ordinary service.

CHAPTER 8

Launching a boat from a trailer—Precautions when stepping the
mast—Parts of the standing rigging—The upper and lower diamonds
—The running rigging—Method of lashing a boat to a trailer—
Floating off—And please leave the slip clear for others.

We are now almost ready to go aboard and I do not doubt
that you are as anxious as I am to be afloat. For however
much pleasure it has been to write of the basic knowledge
that is needed I must own that it will be even more fun to
get down to the actual business of sailing.

We are so close to launching that I think we are justified
in assuming that the boat on her trailer has been backed
down the hard towards the water; that already the small
crowd of watchers has collected (treat them kindly for they
can be of the greatest use if things go wrong); and that
we have chocked the wheels of the car.

It is always worth while to carry eight to ten fathoms of
strong rope of at least two inches circumference, and to
consider that this belongs to the car rather than to the
boat. Launching sites vary enormously in the steepness
of their approach to the water and in only a very few
cases will the angle be such that the trailer can be directly
backed into the sea and the boat floated off without unhitching. And indeed, on the slips where this can be done,
the slope will be so steep that car wheels may well have
insufficient adhesion to pull the boat out over what may
well be a slippery weed-grown surface. Sixty feet of rope
will generally be enough to enable the car to remain
on good ground while the unhitched trailer (secured
to the rope) is lowered gently down the slope using the

towing hitch as a bollard round which to surge the warp.

But before actually unhitching it will be well worth while to step the mast. This is always a delicate operation needing the steadiest platform on which to stand, and that will be while the trailer is still hitched to the car. But here again a word of warning—be sure that there are no overhead wires, either telephone or power, between you and the water, or that if there are they will be well clear of the mast when it is up. Masts are best stepped by being placed on end alongside the boat and then lifted (while still kept upright) by two people standing inside the boat *with their feet on the floor boards.*

The remark in italics is most important. Remember always that a boat is built to take pressure from the outside towards the inside and that great damage may be done if this is reversed, either by walking on the planking when it is unsupported by water, or by allowing rain water to collect in the boat when she is hauled up. This is another point where boats of fibre-glass tend to score over the other constructions. In their case the hull is very nearly as strong one way as the other—not of absolutely equal strength, because, in spite of their pliability, some strength comes from the arch created by the " boat " shape, and this can only work one way.

In some few boats the design is such that the mast, even that for the tall Bermudan rig, can be erected by one man alone, and this, for the father of a family or the single-handed yachtsman, would be a point worth considering in the original choice of a boat. I know that in my own case it could well be a deciding factor. The step of the mast which is designed for single-handed erection is generally so arranged that there is a three-sided box against which the heel of the mast is laid, and then, if you go right aft in the boat, pick up the mast and walk forward at the same time raising the mast at arm's length, the spar will slide

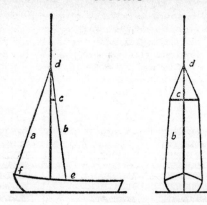

a. *Forestay*   d. *Hounds (where shrouds meet mast)*

b. *Shrouds*   e. *Shroud Plates*

c. *Spreader (optional)* f. *Bow Fitting*

Fig. 26

into place, where it is held by a wooden block or a metal strap.

Assuming that the mast is stepped, we must get the names of the rigging right before we can sail. The wires and ropes that hold up the mast and control the sails are in two parts, the standing and the running rigging. Figs. 26, 27 and 28 will give the names of all the rigging likely to be met with in the boats we are considering.

The greatest strain on a mast comes one third of the way above the deck, and, if it could be conveniently arranged, undoubtedly the spar would be of greater section (and hence stronger) at this point. But masts nowadays are made by machine and, even if the extra expense could be borne, there would still be the problem of arranging that the luff of the mainsail should remain straight. In larger boats one sometimes sees fids of wood strengthening a mast in this area, but that which is more usual in a small boat with a pressing rig and a light mast is to fit extra bracing to the mast (often, because it has less stretch, of very thin stainless steel rod in place of wire). This is called "lower diamond" fig. 27A. Similarly, if the top of the mast needs extra support, it is fitted with an "upper diamond," fig. 27B.

A. LOWER DIAMOND   B. UPPER DIAMOND

Fig. 27

The running rigging is perhaps more varied in particular application between one rig and another, although it should be fairly obvious which name is applicable to whatever rig you have chosen. Fig. 28 gives the names.

There is only one piece which I have not been able to work into the diagram of the running rigging and that is the "tack downhaul" used to secure the lower forward corner of a lugsail (balanced or loose-footed, see fig. 8, B and D). In this rig the yard is hoisted right up by the main halyard

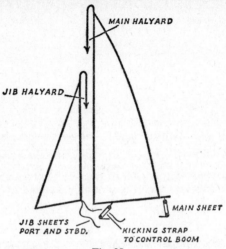

MAIN HALYARD

JIB HALYARD

MAIN SHEET

JIB SHEETS
PORT AND STBD.

KICKING STRAP
TO CONTROL BOOM

Fig. 28

and then the final set of the sail is adjusted by hauling down on the tack downhaul.

Now we can cast off the lashings which have held the boat on the trailer: lashings which should have led from somewhere on the boat (rowlocks set in their plates make excellent lashing points) towards the back of the trailer. See fig. 29. A boat being trailed, because the deceleration of a vehicle being braked is fiercer than the acceleration of the most powerful car, will always tend to slide forward on the trailer.

Then, having made sure that the boat has a bow warp or painter long enough to be reached without getting more wet than you wish, the trailer can be unhitched and the boat run down to the water.

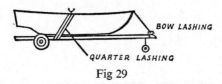

Fig 29

As soon as the boat is afloat the trailer should be taken out of the water. Sea water readily sets up rust and the sealed bearings which the trailer ought to have should not be punished too hard. Of even greater importance, someone else may want to use the slip, and here a word of pleading. Please do see that your car and your trailer are parked well away, where there is no possible chance of their blocking other people's road to the sea. After a long traffic-battled drive there is nothing more infuriating than to arrive at the launching site only to find it completely obstructed by empty trailers hitched to locked and deserted cars whose owners are already far out on the blue waters.

CHAPTER 9

Suiting the sail to be carried to the wind—Preparing to make sail—
Getting the mainsail on the boat—Types of cleat—Setting the jib—
Sailing to windward—The purpose of " luffing "—Balancing the
boat with the crew, who should move steadily and without sudden
movement—Tacking—How to ascertain where you will fetch to on
the new tack—Reaching—Running—Running by the lee—The
unpremeditated gybe—The controlled gybe—Resultant transference of the course line—Precautions when entering harbour with
the wind astern.

After many journeys to look at boats and many more
hours studying particulars, you have your own boat. At
last she is in the water.

Now, with life-jacket on, you can look round at the
weather and decide what sail to carry. It is true that you
could have done this before, but I never feel that the final
decision can be rightly made until the boat is afloat and
her rigging set up. A yachtsman judging the wind's strength
relies to an enormous extent on his ears. In my own boat
I can tell, while I am still in my bunk, what sail I may set
that day by the sound of the wind in the rigging and without
even opening my eyes to look through the scuttle. Even if
this facility is not obtained without practice it is as well to
start realising from the outset whence one's knowledge
comes. Do not be hesitant to reef. With all rigs it is always
more simple, once you are under way, to take out a reef
than to take one in, so lean towards the side of caution.
The more experienced you become the more sail you may
carry with safety. Do not forget that the amount of sail
should be adjusted to suit the crew you have with you on
any particular day. The inexperienced are often dismayed
to find their little platform tipped at an angle of thirty

degrees or more, and that as the mainsail lowers to shut out the horizon they have nothing but swirling waters at which to look.

There is not much point in detailing the various methods by which a sail may be reefed. They are self-evident or will have been described to you by the firm from which the boat was bought. Most modern Bermudan-rigged small boats have their booms so fitted that they can be rotated to roll up the mainsail in exactly the same way that great grandmother rolled up a window blind. The only comment I would make is that where there is no roller reefing and where the sail has a boom, the reef points should not be tied round the boom, but only round the gathered-in roll of sail. To tie them round the boom is to be sure to cause one or two to pull out, because you will not be able to adjust all equally. On the other hand, a sail which is confined by a reef-lacing (a long line passed through a row of reefing eyelets) may have the line passed round the boom because then the individual eyelets can adjust themselves over the whole length of the line.

Reef points should, in small ships, be tied with a reef-bow, not a reef knot. In the smaller sizes of rope the knot is too difficult to undo. To have reef points at all almost certainly suggests that you have a cotton sail, but, should you by chance have one of Terylene which has reef points of the same material, the reef-bow will not stand. It will shake loose. Such reef points may be secured with the full reef knot because the fibres do not shrink when wet and so with them the knot itself will not shrink too tightly to be undone.

Before you hoist the sails be quite sure that the boat is in a position from which you may sail away with ease and decorum. Sir Francis Drake towed his ships out of Plymouth and you may well find it best to row out and pick up some mooring or tie up to a pile or jetty whence the boat will ride to the wind and without interference from the tide or the current. Later on we shall discuss what you should do when such a place cannot be found. For the moment we will assume that you can find somewhere convenient and that the boat is riding to her bow warp, which should be passed through a ring or round a stanchion and brought back aboard so that you may cast this off from inside the boat herself and will neither have to send the crew ashore to do it nor ask them to lean out over the bow to the detriment of the delicate manoeuvre of getting under way.

When riding head to wind get the mainsail up first, making sure that the battens (if fitted) are in their correct pockets and also, if these are held in by little lines, that the cords pass through the eyes in the end of the batten. These points also should be tied with a reef-bow if they are hemp but with a reef knot if they are Terylene.

Before belaying the main halyard make sure that the sliding goose neck fitting has been unlocked. The sail must be hoisted right up and secured before the boom is pressed down at the goose neck and re-locked. It is by this action that the luff should be drawn tight rather than by pulling down on the halyard. This should also be done whenever the sail is reefed or unreefed. It is only too easily overlooked.

As soon as the sail is set to your liking the halyard which hoisted it should be " made up." That is to say it should be coiled neatly in a circle of between 12 and 18 inches depending on the thickness of the rope and the whole tucked under the standing part and pulled home so that half the circle is to each side of the rope that now holds it. It is important that halyards are kept tidily so that, if they have to be let go in a hurry, they may run free. A sail neither up nor down and a piece of " knitting " jammed in the mast-head sheave is a sure prelude to a minor if not a major disaster! When the time comes to let the sail down it is always worthwhile to secure the extreme end of the halyard to a shroud plate or somewhere round the heel of the mast. Nothing looks funnier than someone reaching vainly into the air for the tail of a playful halyard that has almost, but not quite " run away."

It used to be said that no sailor ever put a half hitch over a cleat or belaying pin. But that was in the days when sail was really sail, belaying pins heavy enough to be used as a weapon and cleats measured in foot lengths. In small ships where bodies must necessarily brush the mast I feel that, while this advice still holds for the sheets, it is better to put a half hitch over the halyards so long as there are plenty of turns on the cleat before the half hitch is applied —it will then be easier to shift if spray or rain should shrink the rope. With Terylene or nylon ropes (which are that much more slippery than hemp or cotton) a half hitch will certainly be needed. If you have Terylene sheets you will certainly, for this reason alone, need a set of the lobster-claw jamming cleats.

While the ship has just the mainsail up she will lie quietly enough and, provided there is enough slack in the mainsheet, with only a mild swinging of the boom from side to side. But as soon as the jib is set she will start to fill first on one tack, then the other, and all the time the jib sheets will flog madly. This alone is sufficient reason to do everything possible to reduce the time between having the jib set and getting away.

So lower the centre-board and the rudder (or ship the dagger plate), hoist the jib and make it fast. There will probably be one tack on which you would prefer your ship to start sailing and so you will pull tight the opposite jib sheet to " back " the jib and cause the ship's head to fall off towards the way you wish to go. See fig. 30. As soon as the head begins to swing to starboard release the port sheet and haul in the starboard sheet. The bow will then be free to obey the jib. Haul in the mainboom to suit the chosen course, and then, as soon as the jib is filled by the wind let the sail draw to its proper side.

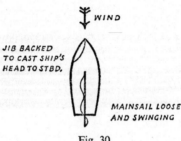

Fig. 30

The next may appear to be a small matter but it is very important and one which you should train yourself to do until the movement is quite instinctive—to see that the mainsheet is ready to run and quite clear of your own feet and the feet of the crew. It is surprising how many accidents arise from the omission to take this simple precaution. To let the mainsheet run is the quickest and simplest way to ease the ship if the wind is too strong. For this reason the mainsheet of an open boat should never be turned up on a cleat but always held in the hand.

Once the boat is sailing you can trim the sails to best advantage by making use of the knowledge we acquired in chapter 4. In that chapter we dealt with the inter-relationship between wind and sails on the assumption that the ship was close-hauled or beating to windward and so, to begin with, we will go on with our imaginary trip with the same supposition. A boat beating to windward makes a series of zig-zags. She can point only as close to the wind as her sails will draw, and on this point of sailing she will make less speed than on any other and her leeway (or the amount she is pushed sideways by the wind) will be greatest. Not many boats will make good a course which is less than 45 degrees from the true wind and only a few will do better than 42½ degrees.

Do not expect too much of your ship by judging her performance in relation to that of other boats which may overtake you. You are not yet as proficient in the art as others, and their ships may well be of a different kind. This is particularly true in comparison with deep-keeled high-performance craft which will not only point much higher than your centre-board boat but will go through the water a deal faster. Everyone is intensely proud of his own ship and the only advice I can give to the chagrined small boat man when he is outpaced by some racing machine is to say to himself " Maybe. But they can't trail the —— thing home! "

Irrespective of this, it is a plain fact that all beginners *will* make the mistake of trying to sail too close to the wind. As we saw in chapter 4, speed through the water alters the relative wind to say nothing of getting the boat somewhere faster. Speed increases the efficiency of the centreboard (and within reason of the whole hull) and cuts down the leeway. You may not be looking as if you were pointing so well; but you will, if you keep the sails really full, be doing a whole lot better.

It will be seen then that if we are to deal with angles measured in half degrees we must be most partciular to see that everything is just as right as we can make it. Most rigs (with headsail and main) go best to windward when the luff of the main (see fig. 31) is just about to

AREA OF "SHAKE"

Fig. 31

" shake "—not a shake that has been induced by a slack leached jib; see fig. 12C. This can be checked by easing the jib sheet to see if in doing so the shake is relieved.

From this shake, extended to the whole sail, has grown the expression and action " to luff," that is to say—to bring the boat momentarily so close to the wind that the sails are all a-shiver. In the short space of time during which the boat will carry her way, and when the sails are freed of the wind, small adjustments to the halyards or sheets can be made more easily than if the force of the wind was still in the canvas. To " luff " is also the first method of easing the ship when she is in danger of being pressed over too far. Only if this simple manœuvre proves insufficient to free the ship should the mainsheet be eased.

The balance of the boat both fore and aft and athwart-ships is important. The crew should be positioned so that the boat is kept as nearly upright as possible. When going to windward it will probably be found best to trim her slightly down by the bow. In effect this means that the crew should be farther forward than when reaching (or beam on to the wind) and again when running before the wind the crew should move aft and trim her slightly by the stern. They will not in effect so trim her. A boat before the wind (from the fact that her mast is forward) will try to bury her nose and, if running hard enough in a big enough sea, may succeed! The movement of the crew towards the stern is to prevent this.

I have said that a boat should always be kept upright and inferred that the helmsman should sit himself on the weather side. But there is just one time when the opposite is true. When ghosting in very light airs it may be possible to get a boat going faster by heeling her away from the weak wind, and for this reason. In these conditions the friction from the wetted surface of the hull will be the greatest resistance to forward motion. Many round-bilged and hard-chine boats will have a smaller wetted area when heeled than when upright. In these conditions I prefer to sail from the lee side of the tiller, from which position I can better see and judge the slot between the jib and the main.

All in all there are few joys in the world to beat the feel of a good boat going well to windward in a smart breeze. The whole delicate machine depends on the hand of one man for its success: even less than a hand, just the finger-tips. The tiller should be as lightly touched as the keys of a piano. Then any sudden movement of the crew can shatter the harmony as surely as the dropping of a piano lid would interrupt a concerto. The crew must be trained to move slowly and in rhythm with the boat's movement—

if they must move at all. Sailing is the essence of quiet motion purposefully pursued by all aboard.

When you have gone as far on the one tack as you wished, or as far as the beach (or some other obstruction) will allow, you will have to put the ship on the other tack. This apparently simple operation can conceal a deal of skill. In fact one can say that the simpler it appears to the onlooker the greater the ability of helmsman and crew. Let us look at it in detail in fig. 32. The first thing is to make certain that everyone aboard knows what is going to happen, and there is no point at all in being bashful about giving orders. You are as much in charge of your own small craft as the captain of an ocean liner is of his very much larger vessel. Give your orders crisply and in the proper language. It is much easier for everybody if you do.

The first order then is " Ready about! " which is a preparative order only and merely serves to draw the attention of your crew. When you are sure everyone has heard, the next order is " Lee-ho! " or " Helm's a-lee! " whichever you like to use. On this order the jib sheet hand lets go the jib sheet while you, the captain, push the tiller gently away from you towards the lee side—fig. 32A.

With the wind still in the main and with the jib eased the boat will begin to come up into the wind and little helm movement will be necessary—probably (depending on the boat) no more than 10 degrees of rudder angle. It is obvious that, when water resistance plays so great a part in preventing forward motion, the less helm we can use the very much better will our turn be, because we shall then not lose the way which the ship has on her. This is going to be important when the turn has been made for reasons we discovered in chapter 4, page 47.

With sails shaking, fig. 32B, the ship is now heading into the wind and, as the whole object is to beat to windward, the further we can " shoot " the boat into the wind's eye the better we shall be doing. This " shooting " should be looked on as a bonus that can be picked up from the disadvantage of having to go about at all. It is a matter of very nice judgment on the part of the helmsman as to how far he can shoot before he must pay out more than he has gained by loss of speed. And this is a judgment which will be valid for only the one occasion. It will depend on wind strength, the size of the waves and the initial speed with which the turn was commenced, and the whole operation can be utterly ruined if the jib sheet hand hauls the jib over too quickly. In fact there is no mistake more frequently made by the inexperienced crew than to haul the jib too soon, very frequently causing it to be back-winded, when it will either cut down the boat's way in the precious moments of shooting or may even cause her to miss the turn and fall back on the tack from which she started.

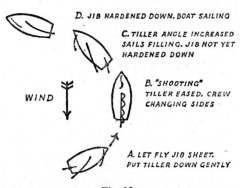

D. JIB HARDENED DOWN. BOAT SAILING

C. TILLER ANGLE INCREASED
SAILS FILLING. JIB NOT YET
HARDENED DOWN

B. "SHOOTING"
TILLER EASED. CREW
CHANGING SIDES

WIND

A. LET FLY JIB SHEET.
PUT TILLER DOWN GENTLY

Fig. 32

During the period of shooting the crew should change sides, moving gently and with precision. To dash across like a football crowd leaving the gates is to shake the ship and utterly ruin the run into the wind's eye. If you want to stop the way on a ship just jump up and down.

In fig. 32C we have her coming out of the turn with the tiller angle increased once more. The mainsail should now be starting to fill with once wind, but, and oh! this is such a big " but," we still do not want that jib to be sheeted down too quickly! The jib sheet hand should grasp the sheet firmly and pull it in with slow precision. We want all those little arrows which we had in chapter 4 to be driving and not heeling forces. If we allow the jib to be suddenly flattened a great heeling force is created. The boat will lean over sharply and additional way is lost both by reason of this increased angle of heel and the worsened presentation of the sails to the wind. Then, as the jib develops its full force once more, the tiller can be eased. The turn is completed and the boat is off on the new tack.

Off to where? And how do you know where we are going to fetch up on the new tack? As a matter of fact there is a very old and well tried method of ascertaining where we are likely to arrive. If a boat is making 45 degrees either side of the wind it will then be obvious (if we think of her and the wind in " plan view ") that on her next tack she will make good a course which would be an extension of a beam bearing when she was just about to tack. If, therefore, we had chosen some thwartship object and looked along it we would have seen where our next tack might be expected to take us.

But, as a matter of fact, it is not quite as easy as that because not all boats make good a course which is 45 degrees from the wind, and some keel boats do quite a bit better. An old fisherman taught me a trick years ago. You sit in the boat with your shoulders parallel to the centreline and, presuming that your boat is a centre-boarder, you look over that shoulder which is nearest the stern and, straining your eyes and your neck as much as is reasonable, you note how far round you can see—and that spot is where you will arrive. But in a keel boat with a good breeze you may turn your head the other way and look over the shoulder which is towards the bow of your ship—and repeat the neck and eye swivel to find out towards what point you can make. No man may see right behind him without turning his shoulders. There is about five degrees of arc over which he cannot make his eyes travel. This, when your shoulders are parallel with the centreline of the boat, represents the difference between $42\frac{1}{2}$ degrees and $47\frac{1}{2}$ degrees off the wind on the new course.

" Reaching " or " being off the wind " covers all those courses which lie between being close-hauled and a course where the ship is so far off the wind that she tends to become more upright again when she can be fairly said to " have the wind free." On these courses it is only a question of trimming the sails to best advantage, and, if comment is to be made, it can only be that after years of sailing with people, many of whom have been comparatively inexperienced, I feel that with the Bermudan rig they have a tendency to ease the sheets more than they should, while with the lug and gaff rig the reverse is the case. On the whole the reach is the easiest sail of them all, so much so that the old sailors coined the phrase " a soldier's wind," inferring, of course, that with such a breeze even a redcoat could hardly get into trouble.

It is a different matter when the wind is really free, and to me this is the most difficult and exacting sail of all. The wind direction (as we will have found in beating to windward) is only very rarely fixed. Each puff must be taken as a separate entity, each change anticipated and, if the wind is heavy enough to warrant doing so, the tiller should be eased and the boat allowed to screw herself to windward. Her wake will then not be a straight line but will be more nearly approximate to a gentle corkscrew as advantage is taken of each puff.

When running, the vagaries of the wind can be very annoying and sometimes dangerous. Fig. 33 explains. With the wind free all is well, but with a dead run the boat will begin to roll and, in doing so, will cause the boom to lift and kick. It is to prevent this movement of the boom that many modern Bermudan rigs are fitted with a " kicking strap " to trice down the boom when it starts this sort of antic. Both the roll and the kicking of the boom will get worse as the wind draws round the same side as that on which the mainsail is set.

When this has happened the boat is " by the lee " and is in danger of " gybing all standing." A heavy unpremeditated gybe in a strong wind may well send the mast

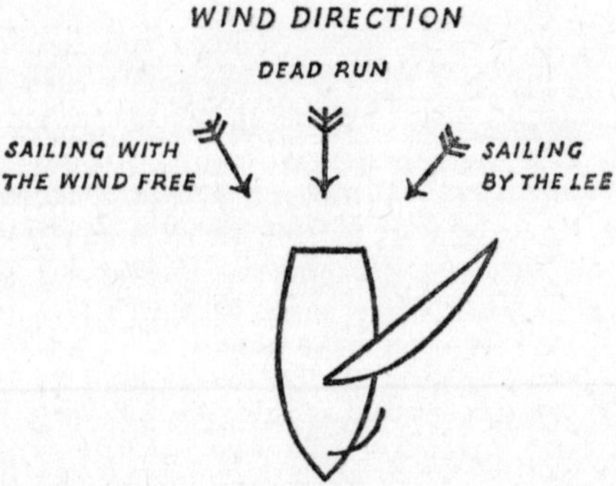

WIND DIRECTION

DEAD RUN

SAILING WITH
THE WIND FREE

SAILING
BY THE LEE

Fig. 33

overboard and so " running by the lee " should be avoided whenever possible, and not only out of regard for the mast: an open boat may well have had her crew lined on what was the weather side. After the gybe and the sudden heel, they will all be to leeward and, being unable to climb back over the inclined hull, their weight may overset the boat. The whole matter is complicated by the fact that many fast planing hulls have marked tendencies to alter course if suddenly heeled. In this sort of racing craft many an unexpected roll has led to a sudden capsize, the boat gybing before the indignant crew have had time to swing themselves inboard.

The difference between racing and sailing in day-sailers is only a matter of the scale of the endeavour. If you are unlikely to overturn your day-sailer, you have to remember that if you handle her badly it is quite possible to do so.

In racing boats intent on saving every half second regardless of safety it is normal practice to raise the centre-board when running because to do so reduces the water resistance, and on a run the question of leeway does not arise. But to raise the board completely is to make the boat harder to steer because the grip on the water is lessened even when the crew have been brought aft to keep the fore-foot high. As the boat will be continually over-taken by waves she has to contend too with their efforts to swing her stern this way and that, and so I feel that she will handle better if some board is left showing beneath the keel. Going down wind in a seaway I like the board to be about a quarter of the way down.

When the skipper realises that his craft is running by the lee he should let everyone else know by singing out " We're by the lee." This is a warning to all aboard that an unpremeditated gybe may take place and is particularly important in small cruisers where the cook may be at the

stove below or some sunning themselves on the foredeck.
Not all bikinis are meant to be unexpectedly ditched! As
far as his own preparedness is concerned, the helmsman
should be ready to push the tiller smartly towards the boom
as soon as he sees it start to swing. But this, I am afraid,
is a council of perfection and of the text book. I don't
remember ever having been able to save a gybe in this way
at so late a time. In strong winds I prefer to carry out the
manœuvre of gybing in the approved and seamanlike
manner.

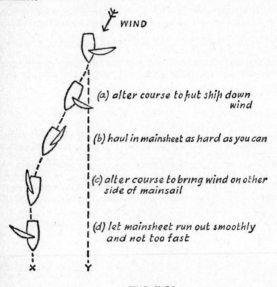

WIND

(a) alter course to put ship down wind

(b) haul in mainsheet as hard as you can

(c) alter course to bring wind on other side of mainsail

(d) let mainsheet run out smoothly and not too fast

THE GYBE

Fig. 34

The proper gybing of a ship requires two hands, and so, to do this, the single-handed yachtsman must learn to work the tiller with his thigh, his shoulder, or some other part of his body so that his hands may be free for the mainsheet.

When a gybe becomes necessary, act as in fig. 34, which, with its notes, is really self-explanatory. The big point to note is that, taking the operation as a whole, there has been an unavoidable transference of the course line from Y to X, and this is going to happen whether the gybe is premeditated or not.

This explains one of the dangers of the dead run which, by the wind's vagaries, can so easily be turned into a run by the lee. It explains, too, why, when entering a crowded harbour, the position is doubly tricky for the simple reason that a transference from Y to X may well take you into a pier or through someone else's topsides.

Certainly at sea, and always when entering harbour, I prefer, if it is at all possible, to zig-zag (or tack) down the wind by gybing the ship first on to the one tack and then on to the other. Or, if this is not possible in close waters, to round the ship to the wind and drop the main with the intention of entering harbour under jib alone: a procedure which is feasible because, if the wind is strong enough for the run to be dangerous, there will be enough to take me in under the single sail.

CHAPTER 10

The return with wind and tide in same direction—With wind and
tide in contrary directions—Picking up a man from the water—
Considerations when coming to anchor—Mooring ship—Getting
under way, wind against tide, with a strong wind, but by a stern
board with a weak wind—Putting a boat on her trailer.

So far in our sailing we have dealt only with what—to
steal a phrase from the cookery books—one might
describe as " good plain sailing." The sauces and flavour-
ings will then be analogous to those quietly made returns
to a fixed position, whether they be to a mooring, a jetty,
or a drowning man, and to the problems inherent in getting
away from more difficult situations than the one we gave
ourselves in the preceding chapter.

I make no sort of apology for the use of the word
" quietly." The essence of skill in sailing is that whatever
is done should not appear to the onlooker to have been
difficult. A ship should move with smooth unhurried
ease to her chosen berth without any shouting. Sails should
fall as if they had been spirited away from the mast by a
magician's wand and then be found to have been gathered
in and secured with a tier by unnoticed hands.

All right. Let us go home, and let us fix ourselves with
a return to a catamaran or jetty under which the tide is
flowing in the same direction as the wind. Unless you can
see the place fully from your approach course it is best to
go in and have a look round and then sail away again
while you make up your mind exactly what you are going
to do. You will of course have the sense to keep up-wind
and up-tide so that both will be in your favour when you

make your approach. So long as there is a sailing breeze, never allow yourself to be afraid of the strength of the tide. A good tide makes everything so much easier because you can still retain steerage way while making little or nothing over the ground.

Never go in to a berth or pick up a mooring without having planned the campaign. While the minutiæ of this must always remain largely in the mind of the master, he would be unwise not to pass the general idea to his crew so that they may know what will be required of them.

Fig. 35 details one method of approach in the circumstances we have supposed. At A we let fly the jib sheet with the intention of taking speed off the boat. Between position A and position B we can sail on the mainsail only, keeping the ship's head steady and using the mainsheet in the same way that we would use the accelerator of

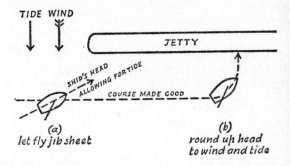

APPROACH WHEN WIND AND TIDE ARE TOGETHER

Fig. 35

a car, keeping the sail full if we want to increase speed for the final rounding up, easing the sheet if we think we are travelling too fast. The same method of approach is applicable whether the point aimed at is a vacant place on the jetty or a mooring buoy in the stream. When we were getting under way we found that, as soon as the jib was set, the boat started to sheer about, and so now, on our return, the first thing to do as soon as the bow warp has been secured is to drop the jib. The main can be got down at leisure.

We will next suppose that the tide and wind are in opposition, the wind being the stronger. Now so long as we have full sail on the boat the wind will be paramount, but as soon as the sail is off we shall be carried back by the tide. Our plan must then be so to act that we shall arrive at our destination at a speed continuously reduced by taking off sail until the point comes when, having no way on her, our boat is a bare inch from her objective with all sail stowed. This should not be difficult. If, after B in fig. 36, you find that the boat has not enough way on her to reach the jetty you can always hoist the jib and keep the halyard in hand until speed has been increased sufficiently to make the objective. Fig. 36 shows how this may be done, and there is little to add except to remark that it is well to give yourself plenty of time, and that it is better to take in the main sooner rather than later. No man may know when a snarl will occur in a halyard, when a batten will foul in the lee rigging or a foot slip. To leave everything to the last minute is to leave it to chance. A seaman must always have something of time or distance in hand—preferably both.

Now these constructions are the only two that are applicable to the berthing of boats. All conceivable situations are either one, the other or some cross between them. Then the necessary action will also be a marriage

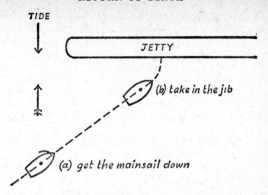

TIDE

JETTY

(b) take in the jib

(a) get the mainsail down

APPROACH WHEN WIND AND TIDE ARE OPPOSED
Fig. 36

of the two methods of approach, with the mind of the master deciding in to whose hands he will finally deliver the ship, the tide or the wind. It will be seen, then, that this last decision must be reached before ever the evolution is begun, and the easiest way of doing this is to observe whether the other boats and yachts in the locality are riding to the wind or the tide. In this connection one has to remember that keeled boats will have a greater tendency to ride to the tide, while shallow draft centre-board boats will ride to the wind. Don't forget that in this respect the positioning of your own centre-board may be made to either hinder or help: centre-board down if you want to swing to the tide: board up if you want to ride to the wind.

The problems of coming smartly to harbour are exactly the same as when you are called on to pick up a man from the water—except that there will then be no tide to worry (or help), for both ship and man will be floating freely on the stream. What is important is that this vital manœuvre should be approached with even more deliberation than berthing. A man disappointed in extremity may collapse and give up; and one hit smartly over the head by the plunging bow will be in no shape to help himself or you. The traditional method of getting a man aboard is to collar him from forward, pass him down the weather side, and get him aboard over the quarter. The weather side is a " must " otherwise the undertow engendered by the ship's leeway will make it impossible for him to be taken aboard at all. The counter is chosen as being the place where in a bigger ship the freeboard is least and where, by reason of a small boat's shape, she has most " bearing " to withstand the sodden weight.

Ideally, and with a rowed boat such as might be dropped from a liner or warship, the rescued man is passed right aft under the oars and hauled aboard over the transom. But in a small sailing boat this will not be possible because the mainsheet would be temporarily fouled by his body. I therefore find no alternative to choose for this manœuvre other than the weather side as far aft as possible *without* interfering in any way with the mainsheet.

The problems of anchoring are still the same as those in figs. 35 and 36, with the intention that when the ship has been brought to a halt in the chosen position she should be just about to make sternway over the land before the anchor is let go. The point of this is to ensure that, as she moves astern over the land, the cable cannot fall in a heap over the anchor and cause it to be fouled. For a small boat there is no more to it than that. Larger boats and cruisers may well wish to anchor for longer periods and in more exposed places and so may lay two anchors out, either by reason of the weather or because by lying between them the swinging room is reduced in a crowded anchorage or narrow channel. This is called " mooring," and fig. 37 explains the reduction in the swinging room.

Some people like to moor with anchors up and down current with the heavier anchor and cable against the strongest run of tide or wind. Some moor with anchors across the stream (termed " with open hawse "). For

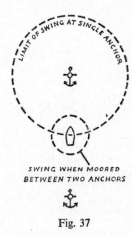

SWING WHEN MOORED
BETWEEN TWO ANCHORS

Fig. 37

myself I choose the first when the tidal effect is likely to be stronger than the wind and the second when the reverse is the case. What *most* matters is that when the two cables have been " middled " they should be tied together and lowered to the bottom so that the weight of chain will keep the pull as nearly horizontal as may be on both anchors.

There now remains only the question of how to get

away from a position less easy than the one we chose for
chapter 9 and then how to get the boat out of the water
and on to her trailer.

We have once more our old problem of wind against tide.
When, in chapter 9, we got under way we made no
assumption about the tide. Had it been flowing approximately in line with the direction of the wind our procedure
would have been the same. But had it been against the
wind and exerted more strength than the wind we could
not have completed the manœuvre as we did.

Fortunately, on most days of good breeze and in most
anchorages round our coasts, small boats tend to lie
wind-rode rather than tide-rode *so long as their centre-
boards are up*. We have here a clue to many simple get-
aways from inherently difficult situations of conflict
between wind and tide. Get the main up to make the ship
ride to the wind and then, as the jib goes up, let go the
buoy rope and do not drop the board until the boat has
payed off on the desired tack.

If the boat is really tide-rode with the wind from
astern, the position is more difficult, for then we can only
get away by reversing the procedure in fig. 36. That is to
say we must first (having prepared everything) let go the
mooring and immediately obtain steerage way by hoisting
the jib. What we do then will depend on many things
inherent in the actual situation. It will be better to suppose
one—see fig. 38—and to work from that. Here we have a
black-hulled small boat lying in the middle of a trot of her
equally small fellows and the whole line is hemmed in by
larger yachts outside. Now if the wind is strong enough to
drive the boat over the tide under jib alone you can run
out on the course marked 1, and then when you reach B1
let go the jib sheet and get your main up with the boat lying
beam on to the wind. This is easily done with the lug or
gunter rig, and most Bermudan mainsails can be hoisted

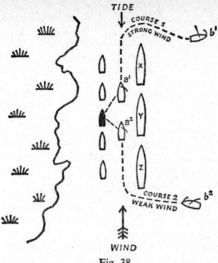

Fig. 38

with the ship beam on to the wind even if they cannot be induced to climb the mast with the wind farther aft.

If the wind is not man enough to beat the tide you will have to make a sternboard. Now this is a perfectly seamanlike operation. With steerage way of any sort you can avoid fixed objects even if you are going stern first over the land. You could even, provided the wind were steady enough, edge sideways to pass between yachts Z and Y. But, if you attempt this, and if Z is a boat sufficiently big to blanket your small sail, you may lose the wind and be driven down upon her. Then, if she has a bowsprit, it will probably pass between your shroud and your mast neatly securing you for an hour or so of hectic labour. Generally speaking it will be better to work your way out at the end of the line towards the position B2 where, clear of immediate danger, you may hoist the mainsail.

There are, of course, other alternatives. You may row the boat to some convenient place out of the main stream of tide, anchor and get your sails up from there. Your own initiative will suggest ways of overcoming the problem: a problem in which personal pride must never be allowed to tempt you to outwit the principles of good seamanship. There are just some things which no wise man attempts. Recognise the impossible and find another way out—to exercise your brains is one of the essential pleasures of sailing. To act otherwise is to invite a muddle and a muck-up, bad language, injured feelings and a damaged boat.

Now to put her back on her trailer. The sails will be stowed away in their bags and the boat " made up " tidily. The trailer is run down to the water, the car backed down to the limit of good ground traction for the tyres, and the rope is led from the trailer hitch to the car with a clove hitch over the ball. It is important that it is the car end of the rope which can be tied and untied quickly. Then the trailer is put down into the water and the boat rowed on and secured with her bow warp. With a driver in the car and one assistant at the trailer, the car is started. The assistant takes the weight off the draw bar of the trailer both to prevent the jockey wheel digging in and to help in guiding the trailer past any obstruction there may be. Piles of lobster pots, old boats and odd bits of flotsam seem to encumber all our launching sites!

When the car has gone as far as is convenient, the trailer wheels are chocked and the car run backwards to the limit of the good ground. The rope is then shortened and the procedure repeated—again and again, until the trailer with its boat can properly be hitched to its car. Then the boat is lashed down, the mast taken out and secured in the towing position. With a good assistant I can put one of our boats in the water from the hard we use—which is not as easy as some—in seven minutes and take her out in ten. It is really not much time out of a day.

CHAPTER 11

The uniform system of buoyage—A large scale chart should be available and a prior visit to the launching site at low water is desirable—The markings on a chart—Going aground—Procedure for getting off—Some boats draw most water when upright, some when heeled—Laying out an anchor to warp off—Never try to walk a boat off—Rules for preventing collision at sea—The starboard bow, the dangerous quadrant—Insurance; the need for third party cover—Navigation lights for small vessels—Sound signals.

So far we have omitted all reference as to where we can go on the water and what action we should take if we meet any other yacht or vessel on a course where there will be a collision if one of us does not alter.

The channels of the sea are marked by a uniform system of buoyage and it will be very well worthwhile to study this and have it by heart. Likewise it is absolutely necessary to have a complete knowledge of the simple rule of the road.

In this country the shape of a buoy is more important than its colour (although the colour will in nearly every case be found to conform to rule). Can-shaped, and generally red buoys with red lights, should be left on the sailer's port side when going with the main stream of flood tide. Conical, and generally black, buoys with white lights are left on the starboard hand when going with the flood. The pylons or perches marking the channels to the more important of the smaller ports are similarly painted—red pylons to port when entering harbour, black to starboard. When they are lighted, these marks carry the same colour of light as the corresponding buoys. In those creeks which are too small to have pylons the channels are marked by perches (or old poles) on which, for the port hand marks, white crosses are nailed, while those to be left on the starboard hand remain bare. But in these very small places great care must always be taken. The crosses may have blown off in past gales and the perches themselves may either have fallen over or been carried away by visiting yachts and not replaced.

Just occasionally, and where there is an old tradition of yachting and an even older and entirely British tradition of non-conformity, you will find some small port which has an entirely original system of marking the poles that define the meandering waterway which leads the inquisitive small boat enthusiast up its twisty channel. Then you may suddenly come upon a basket on the port-hand pole and a tar barrel on the starboard, but sailing directions published by the yachting press generally exist for these places and anyway they are usually self-evident.

The approach to a channel from seaward is marked by a fairway buoy. These buoys are large and always have a high lattice top mark so that they may be sighted at a good distance. They are painted with black and white or red and white vertical stripes but, as they are lonely characters, there is little chance of a mistake in their identity. At the entrance to some smaller undredged channels there are buoys marking the bar. They are normally conical and red with the word BAR in white letters. They are generally so sited that provided you have a chart their purpose is self-evident.

Middle-ground buoys—that is buoys which mark a bank which lies in the middle of the channel and divides it temporarily into two separate waterways—are spherical and painted in black and white horizontal stripes if the main channel is to the *left* when going with the flood tide: spherical and painted in red and white horizontal

(A) FAIRWAY AND MID-CHANNEL BUOYS

(B) MARKS TO BE LEFT ON THE PORT HAND GOING WITH THE FLOOD TIDE

CAN BUOYS (generally painted RED, RED and WHITE) RED POSTS, PERCHES WITH TOP MARKS

(C) MARKS TO BE LEFT ON THE STARBOARD HAND GOING WITH THE FLOOD TIDE

CONICAL BUOYS (generally painted BLACK, BLACK and WHITE) BLACK POSTS, PERCHES WITH NO TOP MARKS

(D) MARKS TO BE LEFT ON EITHER HAND

| SPHERICAL BUOYS and POSTS painted RED, WHITE, BLACK, indicate ISOLATED DANGER | SPHERICAL BUOYS and POSTS painted BLACK and WHITE, MIDDLE GROUND MAIN CHANNEL TO LEFT | SPHERICAL BUOYS and POSTS PAINTED RED and WHITE, MIDDLE GROUND MAIN CHANNEL TO RIGHT |

Fig. 39

114

stripes if the main channel is either to the *right* or when both channels are of equal importance. Middle-ground pylons are painted black and white when the main channel is to the left of them: red and white when it is to the right or when both are equal. There is always a mark at both ends of a middle ground.

Isolated dangers are marked by spherical buoys painted with horizontal red, white and black stripes, or by pylons painted with bands of the same sequence.

Spoil-ground buoys are yellow and indicate places where dredgers dump silt and garbage boats deposit refuse. It is not good ground in which to anchor.

Watch buoys, by which lightships check their position in bad visibility, are small, can-shaped and red with the word WATCH painted in white on their sides. As these are unlighted the possibility of their presence suggests that lightships should not be approached within a cable (two hundred yards) at night for, though small, these buoys are big enough to make a nasty gash in a yacht.

The indication of wrecks produces yet another series of markings. Wrecks which are dangerous to shipping will generally have run aground on one side or other of the channel, and so we have the shape, can or conical, coming up again to tell us on which side they should be passed. Leave can-shaped green buoys, with the word WRECK in white letters, to port, conical ones to starboard, when going with the flood. A green post in a small channel should be self-explanatory. There remains only the problem of the wreck-marking vessel. This ship is as big as a light vessel and will be used only in very large channels or the open sea. The safest answer, then, is to keep well away (at least two cables) from her because, however big a vessel the wreck may have been, it cannot have been longer than three hundred and thirty yards (1,000 feet). A " cable " is a nautical distance of 200 yards, a tenth of a sea mile, and so " two cables distance " will keep us clear.

Summing up, we get this table:

WHEN GOING WITH THE FLOOD TIDE

To be left to Port.	To be left to Starboard.
Can buoys.	Conical buoys.
Red posts.	Black posts.
Perches with crosses.	Plain perches.

To be left on either hand.
Spherical buoys.
Red-, white- or black-banded posts.

To guide you to a channel.
Fairway buoy.
Bar buoys.

To be avoided like the plague.
Wreck buoys.
Spoil-ground buoys.

To make sense of any water in which you intend to sail it is well worth while to buy a large-scale chart of the area. The small cost can save a deal of tribulation. It will also be of great help to have made a previous journey to the launching site at low water. Then you will have seen the more immediate dangers. Or, if this is impracticable, at least you should plan your first visit to a new area of activity so that you and your boat arrive when the tide is low. It is amazing what a difference there is in the look of a place between the time when all the banks and obstructions can be seen and the time, but a few hours later, when a gentle wind-ruffled blue surface mockingly covers the hidden dangers.

When you have bought your chart it is worth giving it a little study. First you must check the chart datum to which level the soundings have been reduced. This will be clearly stated in the " title." By international agreement the chart datum is at a plane below which the tide seldom falls. On British charts this is usually just below the level of Mean Low Water Springs for the area. It can be assumed then that the water will never normally be less than the depth shown. (For remarks on extra-ordinary tides see chapter 12.) On some charts, mainly those of smaller scale, the depths are in fathoms; on charts of larger scale they are generally given in feet— the title tells you in which measure the depths have been made. Figures which are underlined indicate the banks which show at low water and the figure is the height at which they dry out above chart datum. This underlined figure *is always given in feet* irrespective of the measure used for the depths in the offing.

Of course you will go aground. This can hardly be helped. The charted positions of the banks are, in small rivers and estuaries, only very rarely brought up to date and there is always the chance that silting or erosion will have made quite a difference to the channel. The perches and withies should keep you clear, but one may be missing and we always have to contend with the swirls of the tide and the fickleness of a wind which will sometimes delight in driving us into taking a seamanlike chance and then die away to leave us to get out of the mess as best we may. Oh, you'll go aground all right!

The point to realise is that, for a centre-board boat exploring the delightful creeks and shallows of our coast, this going aground is just an occupational hazard, and you must be quite ready with a drill that will get you off again without too much exertion.

If the centre-board is down, its warning chattering as it

touches the ground should be sufficient warning. Then by raising the board and making a quick turn back to the known deep water you should get free of the shoal. But unfortunately it sometimes happens that the tide is setting right across the shallow patch and then, as you raise the board, you are carried farther and farther up the bank.

The golden rule is I think that if she does not come off at the first attempt, then get the sail off her. I know that hastily dropped sails do clutter the boat, but on the other hand I feel that, unless the wind is strongly off the shore on which you have grounded, to keep them up is always bad tactics because it introduces another imponderable in allowing the wind's antics to interfere with your getting free.

With the sail off and with oars used to push her head round, you ought to be able to get away again unless the tide is falling very fast. Being familiar with your boat, you should know whether she will draw least water when up-right or when heeled. Most round-bilged boats with a keel can be made to draw between two and three inches less by heeling them through 10 or 15 degrees, and this is partic-ularly applicable to small cruisers with a centre keel, when the reduction in draught due to one man standing on the gunwale and holding on to the shrouds may be nearly nine inches or even a foot. Observe that to do this would not be safe if the sails were still set. Observe too that, unless you are very certain of the quality of the bottom, it is never a good idea to put a man over the side. Many of our rivers have banks of mud of a consistency which, though strong enough to prevent a ship's movement, will not support the weight of a man. If someone gets caught thigh deep in this sort of mud he will be just another problem to solve and only add to the consternation aboard.

While we are talking of mud, if you should get stuck in it and feel yourself sinking or if, after a capsize, you find that the bank to which you have swum is too soft to support the weight of your feet, lie down on your belly and try to work yourself forward like a frog.

To return to the boats. A hard-chine boat will draw least water when she is upright, and so too will one of the small cruisers which have twin bilge keels. This last type of boat can *increase* her draught by anything up to nine inches when heeled and so these craft must be brought upright when attempting to release them from the ground —yet another case where dropping the sails is an advantage. If the tide is falling and the boat will not come off there is nothing to do but wait for the tide to return. If the tide is rising, lay out an anchor and wait. If the ground is firm you can carry the anchor some way towards the deeper water, then the moment the boat floats she can be hauled off. It is unwise when the tide comes back to attempt to walk the boat into deep water. There are people who have been left behind on a bank and have had to swim after their boats—sometimes a thankless task and always a dangerous one. After a long swim it is not easy to haul yourself aboard unless there is someone to help you.

Briefly the motto for going aground is this: " Get the sail down, stay in the boat."

The more than 30 articles which comprise the *International Regulations for Preventing Collisions at Sea* can, for our purpose, be very greatly condensed. The basic rules are extremely simple. The main rule is enshrined in article 29 which I shorten to read, " Nothing in these rules shall exonerate any vessel from neglecting the ordinary practice of seamen, or the special circumstances of the case." In other words, when the whole intricate structure cast in legal phraseology has been boiled down and passed through the sieve of common sense we are left with these simple rules:

1. *When navigating a narrow channel keep to the starboard side and pass other vessels coming the other way port to port.*

2. *Have a sense of proportion and keep out of the way of all large steamers and yachts much larger than yours.*

3. *Make any alteration that will be necessary to your own course in plenty of time so that the other fellow can see your intention clearly. The officer of a big steamer travelling fast has to think much farther ahead than you do. You will have been in the wrong if you have held on to your course long enough for him to have had any thought of " what the hell you are up to." It is true that by tradition steam gives way to sail—but not that much, although motor yachts can and should be expected to do this.*

4. *Subject again to the comment on disparity in size, the overtaking vessel should always keep clear of the one she is trying to pass.*

Then, as far as the meeting of sailing boats of your own size is concerned there are the following rules. The new racing rules have slightly altered the traditional regulations but these apply only to yachts actually engaged in racing. It would be pointless to detail the divergencies in this volume, as it is understood that they are soon to be altered once more. If you race you'll find out—and racing, as I have said before, is now a separate form of the sport.

5. *A yacht running free keeps out of the way of one close-hauled.*

6. *A yacht close-hauled on the port tack keeps clear of one on the starboard tack.*

7. *When both are running free with the wind on different sides the one which has her boom to starboard keeps clear.*

8. *When both are running with the wind on the same side, the boat to windward keeps clear.*

A yacht proceeding under auxiliary power (even an open boat with an outboard motor pushing her along) should behave as if she were a fully-powered vessel and the rules for her are as follows.

9. *When two vessels are meeting head on, each should alter so that they pass port to port (as in the river).*

10. *When two vessels are crossing so as to involve risk of collision, the vessel which has the other on her starboard side shall keep out of the way.*

So much for the ten golden rules for safety at sea, which are already the digest of many pages, but although I have so set them out, they can be condensed even further. They can be brought down to the two simple facts: that if you meet with any other vessel which is on a collision course with you and which appears from your own ship to lie between your starboard beam and right ahead, then it is your duty to keep clear, and that a yacht running keeps out of the way of one that is close-hauled.

To these two there can be only one small doubt. My rules 7 and 8 deal with the problem of which ship should give way when both are running. Now this is one of those strange regulations which administrators have from time to time to make in order to stop a loophole in some other order. Consider the situation carefully and you will see that it is *most* unlikely that both ships will be travelling at the same speed. One will be overtaking the other and so the " overtaking " rule applies. Rules 7 and 8 need never have been written except to cover this one unlikely event.

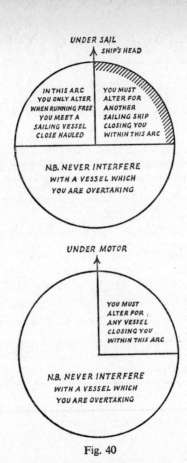

Fig. 40

In reducing our " dangerous corner " to the starboard bow, we can make one important deduction. We now see that when we are on the port tack and sailing hard the foot of the jib may obscure our vision over much of this arc. It behoves us therefore to be more than ever cautious when on the port tack to look under the jib to see that all is well. And please do not forget that in a stiff breeze it will be equally difficult for any other small boat master on that tack to see his own dangerous arc. If, then, you see that the other fellow is unaware of your presence it is only common courtesy to go about (or go under his stern) rather than to hang on, risk a collision and shout " What the hell do you think you're doing ! " After all, it might well have been you, and you *are* bound by article 29, " or special circumstances of the case," to do your utmost to prevent collision at sea.

Talking of collision, do not forget to insure your boat, her trailer and, of course, to arrange third-party cover both at sea and on the road. The third-party cover should be very high, at least £25,000 (it does not cost a great deal) because even the smallest boat can incur the most enormous bill for damages, not so much by the hurt it can do to others as by blocking a channel or lock gate and so interfering with commerce—then the charges of demurrage roll in and are backed by the cost of lifting the wreck.

As you are, I feel, unlikely to sail at night, no mention has been made of navigation lights—nor in any case are they at all necessary, or even desirable. The small lights (which are all that the average yacht can show) are virtually useless in anything but perfect weather. When the yacht is heeled by the wind one light points up above to St. Peter's gate and the other to the Devil down below, and neither gentleman has, as yet we hope, the slightest interest in the imminence of your arrival. Article 7, sub-section 4, contains the answer. It reads " Small boats, whether under oars or sail, shall only be required to have ready at hand a lighted lantern showing a white light which shall be temporarily exhibited in sufficient time to prevent collision."

You will not, of course, have to go to sea with a lighted lantern! The modern torch has arrived since the days when the regulations were drawn up. But the suggestion is there—and it is an excellent answer: the largest and most powerful torch you can afford to carry, and the method of its use is important. On the too close approach of a steamer or other vessel, shine the torch in the direction of his bridge for a period of about one minute to attract his attention to your presence. During this minute you will have time to make an appreciation of the situation and to decide what you are going to do about it, using the same consideration (and perhaps a bit more) that you would give to a big vessel by daylight. If you decide to alter your course you should then switch off the light, make the alteration, and then expose the torch once more but this time the beam should be directed upon your own sails.

The floodlit sails of a yacht (particularly those of Terylene) can be seen at a very great distance, fully two miles, but what is of prime importance is that the officer of the watch on the liner can then see exactly what course you are steering and take action accordingly. The light should be kept on your sails until all chance of collision is passed.

If then, there is any chance of your not returning before dark, it is advisable to arm yourself by taking a good torch with a strong beam along with you.

Lastly, the sound signals that a steamer may make to you. They are not just rude noises to clear a way for her passing. The code is this:

One short blast means " I am altering my course (the steamer's) towards my starboard hand."

Two short blasts means " I am directing my course towards my port hand."

One long blast says " I am here and what are you going to do about it? " But with this signal there may often be a misunderstanding. Perhaps from the natural courtesy of one sailor to another, or possibly due to the fact that masters of passenger vessels hesitate to harry the eardrums of their customers at the same time that they soak their clothes with steamy spray from the siren, this warning may be so perfunctorily made that it can be mistaken for the one *short* blast. It is a point worth remembering: that if you hear only one blast it is as well to watch the bow of the steamer carefully. It may swing to starboard to clear you. It can come straight on.

CHAPTER 12

Reefing—In rough water this will appear to be necessary earlier than when under the lee of the land—Danger of approaching big vessels anchored in the fairway—Procedure for reefing—The use of transits in keeping track of where the boat is—Righting a boat after a capsize—The structure of waves and their behaviour in shoal water or when faced with a tide—The effect of tides on cruising radius—Of tide on the apparent wind—The varied rise and fall of the tide at various ports, and the consequences.

When the wind becomes too powerful you will have to reef. If the ship is at sea this point will appear to be reached sooner than if she is under the lee of the land, for then the waves of themselves will intermittently increase the relative heeling of the boat in relation to the water surface. I wrote " appear to be reached " with a purpose, because I believe that, pleasant though it may be for the expert to overdrive a small boat in a strong wind and smooth water, it is not a good game for the novice.

Under the lee of the land the wind can be extremely gusty, and the flurries do not behave as do the true squalls of the sea. Very often they come from between high buildings or down the sides of piers, warehouses or cliffs. Their direction will then be out of truth with the real wind and so the small boat may have to contend not only with the sudden increase in the wind strength but a vicious change in its direction which, catching the boat on the beam while her sails are close trimmed, will heave her down. Again, where at sea the wind is parallel to the surface and the approach of a gust can be seen on the water before it hits you, the direction of the wind under the lee of the land is often downward and may strike without any visible warning of its approach.

126

Fig. 41A shows the effect of a typical gust with the wind already inclined downwards so that the normal easing that a ship may achieve by the incline of her sails will afford her little or no relief.

Fig. 41B shows an effect which may be experienced on the weather side of a cliff or building where the wind (although apparently as strong as ever all round you) may suddenly " lift " to leave you floundering in a seaway and in danger of being driven ashore by the send of the sea. Both these situations can also be found close to the sides of big merchantmen anchored or moored in a channel. Big ships at anchor tend to ride more to the tide than to even quite a strong breeze and so may well be lying mainly across the wind. You can be sure however, if the steamer is moored to a buoy at both ends with the wind on her beam, that the mooring chains will be lying out at an angle to her hull. If then you lose control of your boat the tide will take you along her side and your mast may well catch the cable that holds her to the buoy. Stay well away from big steamers at anchor unless you have a leading wind.

Gusts coming down over buildings or cliffs strike the water and fan out, (fig. 41). This means that, if the centre of the gust is to pass ahead of you, the wind you feel in the gust will appear to " head " you, while if the centre of the gust passes astern the reverse will be the case. From this we see that an advantage can be seized. Where a gust passes astern you should be able, by bringing the ship closer to the wind, to steal a few yards to windward for every second the gust lasts. It can make a lot of difference in a fierce beat home over a strong tide.

All in all I think that until you feel fully confident of your boat handling you should reef sooner rather than later wherever you are, if only because it is much more easily done before the matter is forced upon you.

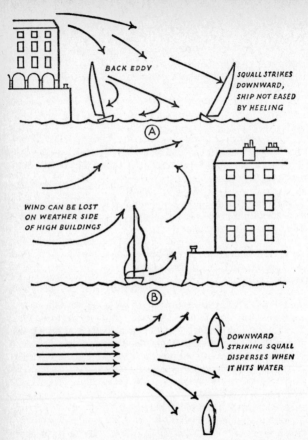

BACK EDDY

SQUALL STRIKES DOWNWARD, SHIP NOT EASED BY HEELING

Ⓐ

WIND CAN BE LOST ON WEATHER SIDE OF HIGH BUILDINGS

Ⓑ

DOWNWARD STRIKING SQUALL DISPERSES WHEN IT HITS WATER

Fig. 41

The important thing, then, is to see that the boat is under control all the time. This is best achieved by taking in a roll and then giving the boat (and yourself) a breather: the boat a chance to recover her steerage way, and her people to look around and see that they still have uncluttered sea room in which to complete the manœuvre.

Proceed as follows. First see that the fall of the main halyard is off its pin or cleat and clear to run. Then ease up the tack clamp of the gooseneck and let it ride up to the top of its track. The helmsman should then ease the sheet a little until the sail is not fully drawing but is still held by the wind, and he must do his utmost to hold the boat on this course during the next phase. The crew then lets out a foot or so of the main halyard and takes a turn. Then, by easing the heel of the boom from the squared portion of the gooseneck, he rotates the boom until he has rolled up as much as he can of the sail.

When as much as possible of the slack sail has been rolled up, the helmsman hauls in the mainsheet and gets the boat sailing again. The sail will not be of a perfect set but it should be good enough to drive her forward once more. The process is then repeated until enough turns have been rolled in. It is possible (indeed it is probable) that the leach will not have ridden smoothly round the rotated boom, but this " little by little " method of reefing has the advantage that the helmsman can probably luff the boat up during the sailing periods and, reaching for the end of the boom from where he sits, haul the sail taut. With the tack clamp not set up and the luff not over-tight, the boom end will be lower in the boat than when the sail is properly set.

When enough rolls have been turned in, the main halyard is hauled as taut as possible and then the gooseneck is pressed hard down in its track once more and the tack clamp fixed.

Here a word to help you keep abreast of the overall situation in moments when so much is happening in your own boat that it is only too easy to overlook what wind and tide have done to you in the few moments since you last had a thought to spare. The best method of checking your movement over the sea when you are in close contact with the land is by transits: that is to say by the movement of one object which is near at hand against an object some way off. Anything will do; a mast against a tree; a pier against a church tower, even a sea bird asleep on one leg against a clump of seaweed. If you get into a habit of noting these transits as they come and go you will soon be able to keep a constant, almost sub-conscious, check on how much the boat has moved during the moments when she has required all your attention.

Let me emphasise right away that one does not expect a boat to capsize. The normal displacement hull of stable midship section is more likely to fill and sink than turn over, and anyway some action should be taken to prevent this happening long before disaster occurs. I have never in my life capsized or sunk a sailing boat. On the other hand, light displacement hulls of planing form driven hard by racing crews may in good sportsmanship take risks which are not to be related to normal seamanship. They can and may be driven to capsize.

If provided with adequate buoyancy, the modern boat will not sink and the problem then will be to get her upright again. For some considerable time the boat will probably lie on her side and during this period she may be fairly easily righted. Indeed if both the crew could get their weight on the centre-board and hold on to the gunwale which is above the water she would probably come up. The problem then would be to keep her there while she was still full of water. A flooded hull will have its stability greatly reduced and, if the wind was enough to

130

turn her over when she was empty, it will certainly lay her flat again before an attempt can be made to board her. The sail *must* be got down before the boat is righted.

This job at the mast can be done by one man while the other is on the centre-board. In these conditions it will not be safe for one to work at the base of the mast unless he is assured that the boat will not turn right over and float with mast downwards, imprisoning him beneath her —hence the need to send the crew round to control any such tendency by holding down on the centre-board. Then, with one of the crew having shouted his presence at the board, it will be quite safe for the other (supported by his life jacket) to attack the base of the mast, let go the halyard, get the jib down and unhanked from the forestay and the mainsail out of the luff groove on the mast.

When the sail is off her both men may get on the centre-board and right the boat. Assuming the boat to have been racing and so under the eye of a committee, help should by now have arrived with buckets with which to bale out. But whether these are available or not there may well be some difficulty in preventing water re-entering as fast as it is put out. Not only will the boat be low in the water and so subject to seas coming over the lowered side, but water may come up through the slot in the top of the centre-board case, and this may have to be plugged with socks, trousers or soft gear of some sort before success is achieved.

Contrary to what is often believed, the centre-board is not there to enhance the stability of a small boat and will not do so unless it is of a very heavy gauge of iron or steel. Its function is to prevent the boat slipping to leeward and, while it is true that it offers a resistance to what might be termed the " swaying motion " by its area underneath the boat, it will be obvious from fig. 42 that when the board is doing its job of preventing leeway the pressure on the lee side must be greater than that on the other and so

HEELING MOMENT OF CENTREBOARD

Fig. 42

the resultant lever will be a capsizing rather than a righting moment.

The management of a small boat in a big sea is largely a matter of nerve and experience. The sea itself is neither cruel nor kind, it is just supremely indifferent. Fortunately, however, it is subject to certain physical rules which it cannot disobey. The water in a wave does not move, the surface bends and then falls flat again. It is like a mouse running under a cloth: the hump moves, the cloth remains stationary. When a wave gets so big that the top loses equilibrium it breaks, but so long as the wave is undisturbed it quickly regains its lost equilibrium and the spume of the burst slides harmlessly down its back.

It follows therefore that a small boat in deep water can live in surprisingly big seas. In all normal weather trouble comes only when the water ceases to be deep or when a tide is running into the seas. Both of these postulates can create dangerous conditions. Then the waves are driven up far beyond their point of equilibrium. The crests turn over and roll forward as moving water. The bad weather rule, then, is to keep always in the deepest possible water and to avoid sailing in areas where a strong tide is running into the face of the sea.

Tides affect all who go down to the coast to sail or motor their boats, and their effect is enormous. Twice every day fantastic quantities of water flow through our harbour entrances and up our rivers; while backwards and forwards in the channels and round our islands wash the enormous water gradients of the tide. To set out to fight this phenomenon is just a waste of time. Consider that if your boat is making four knots through the water and you have a two-knot tide with you, you are making six knots over the ground. But if you have the same tide against you the resultant speed over the ground will be reduced to two knots. In the first instance you will be going three times as quickly towards your destination as in the second.

We did however, in the second case, suppose that the boat was on a steady course stemming the tide. Had the wind been such that you had been trying to beat against the tide, the result would have been different. A boat beating to windward cannot expect to progress on her mean course at any speed much greater than half her speed through the water, for she cannot make good a course closer than 45 degrees to the wind. If, then, we are making four knots through the water we shall only be making half that, two knots, on course. So if there is a two-knot tide you will not be moving over the ground at all!

Many people have a surprising difficulty in allowing for the set of a cross tide to their course. If you watch the racing boats beating up to a mark against a cross tide you will see that for every helmsman who steers a steady course to round the buoy two others will either overlay the mark or make insufficient allowance for the set and will have, at the last moment, to make another tack. I once had considerable success with one man I was teaching by

133

asking him to imagine the water as stationary and to consider the buoy as an object moving through the water! It worked, and perhaps, for we all see natural phenomena in different ways, it may help others to look at it in that light.

The tide can also greatly affect the apparent wind. If the tide is running into the wind the apparent wind speed will be the sum of the two velocities whereas if the wind and tide are the same way the speed of the tide should be subtracted from the other. Wind in normal sailing weather is not so very fast.

WIND FORCE 1 is 1— 3 m.p.h.
2 is 4— 7 m.p.h.
3 is 8—12 m.p.h.
4 is 13—18 m.p.h.

Now if we assume a wind speed of ten miles per hour which will give us a nice gentle sail, and we have a two-knot tide sliding the whole surface towards the direction from which the wind is blowing, the apparent wind will be twelve miles per hour: while if both had been flowing in the same direction the apparent wind could only be eight miles per hour, and the difference between eight and twelve is quite significant.

This effect of the tide on the wind can make a difference in another practical way: fig. 43 explains. In that example we have assumed that we are trying to get out of a harbour into which the tide is flowing. It is half flood and the tide is running its strongest. We have, however, been doing pretty well, for, by hugging the eastern arm of the land we have been able to cheat the tide and have even had some advantage from a tidal eddy. We are now at A, close-hauled on the starboard tack, and aboard the boat everyone is sure that we shall be able to break out. But shall

134

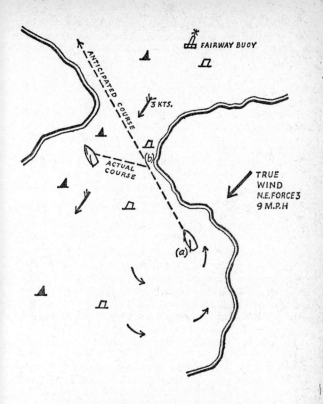

EFFECT OF TIDAL STREAM ON APPARENT WIND
Fig. 43

135

we? Not a bit of it! As soon as we reach position B we shall run into the full strength of the tide and at that very moment when we most want a good wind we shall suffer a reduction of three knots in its speed (which is the equivalent to three and a half miles per hour). This will reduce the apparent wind speed from nine to five and a half miles per hour; and it is absolutely impossible to beat against a three-knot tide with a wind which is no better than five and a half miles per hour.

Tides do not only go backwards and forwards, they go up and down; and by how much they do so varies a great deal from place to place. While in general it can be said that the tides of the west coast have a greater range than those of the east, there are a great many anomalies which make any rule of thumb impossible. Tide (which after all is only a very big wave) behaves just as any other water will do. Tides have a momentum of their own, and, like water washed up the sloping end of a bath, they will expend their momentum in raising themselves when they are restricted as at the sloping end of a bath. Tide has a velocity which is fixed within certain limits, and so with one part of the tidal wave having to go round Scotland and the other up the English Channel, it will not have time to fill up the east coast before the receding wave of the main tide draws the waters back again.

Fortunately, as the whole tidal effect is mainly dependent on the phases of the moon (and to some extent of the sun) its comings and goings can be accurately predicted many months, if necessary years, ahead. The combined effect is to produce a difference in the tidal range which gives us a higher tide than the mean (called " Springs ") and a lower tide than the mean (called " Neaps ") at approximately 15 days interval between each spring tide and, of course, the same period between neaps. The tides on the intervening days will be higher or lower depending on whether you are approaching the maximum low of neaps or the spring peak.

It will be seen, therefore, that if you were to go ashore in a heavy boat at the top of a spring tide you might well be there for a fortnight—and this has happened.

Because of this it will be well worth while to study the local tide table before you venture forth in your boat, and if you are going to trail to various places (which would appear to be the great attraction of trailing) then you should buy one of the Nautical Almanacs for the year. For the ordinary yachtsman Reed's is the best because it contains in one volume such a great deal of other useful data. Even if this is not of immediate import you will find it interesting, and on the inevitable day when you decide to buy a larger boat you will find the store of knowledge more than useful.

The rise of the tide in the area you intend to work is of paramount importance, perhaps even more so than its speed in the channel or offing. Consider the table below which gives the height of the spring tides at various ports.

West		*East*	
FALMOUTH	18′	DOVER	20′
CARDIFF	40′	BURNHAM	18′
LIVERPOOL	30′	HULL	21′
GLASGOW	12′	NEWCASTLE	15′

Now, however great the range of the tide may be, it has to make its rise in six consecutive hours and its fall in the same period. Like the hand-made wave in the bath, water starts slowly, reaches a maximum velocity, stands for a moment and then starts to fall back slowly; then for a period it moves more quickly again, until, nearing the end of the cycle, it once more slows down. The rate of the rise and fall of the tide in the first hour after slack water is approximately one twelfth of the total range, one sixth during the second hour, a quarter during each of the third and fourth hours, one sixth again in the fifth hour, to finish with the final twelfth in the last hour.

The practical application of the preceding paragraph is this: that during the third hour of the ebb at Cardiff the tide will fall ten feet, while at Newcastle (and during the same period of the tide) the fall would be only three feet nine inches. In other words, if you are to go aground you will have to act just three times as quickly off Cardiff as you will off Newcastle if you are to have the same chance of getting the boat off the bank.

Again, if the crew of a yacht wish to go ashore in the dinghy for dinner at Cardiff when the tide is on the ebb, and leave their boat secured to the steps of the sea wall, they will need a very long painter!

I have said that tides can be accurately predicted, and so they can, but this is only on a theoretical basis. The weather (the barometric pressure and the direction and force of the wind) can cause them sometimes to " cut " and sometimes to " surge " by quite a few feet, and naturally this may alter the rate of the stream in narrow channels. The data given in the tide tables can therefore be taken only as an approximation, for no man may foretell the weather far enough ahead for its effect to be tabled.

From all this chat about tides it might be supposed that they are the main bugbear which the sailor must face going out in his ship to the sea. This is not so: certainly not for the man who can be punctual, even at four o'clock in the morning. By their aid you can increase the range of your sailing enormously. Anyone who has sailed the tideless waters of the Baltic or Mediterranean will know the full force of that dictum! Fail to arrive on time, miss the tide and your day is only a " might have been."

CHAPTER 13

A question of balance—The personal waves of a boat—An experiment to determine the altered trim of a boat as she is heeled—Constant concentration demanded of the helmsman—The balance of the sails (on the wind and down the wind)—The effect of the waves of the sea, which travel too fast to be escaped—The matter of the helmsman's bodily balance; can be developed by the position of his body—Why a boat that is running may " broach to "—Matching the rhythm of the ship to that of the waves.

Now that we have discussed the function of the sails and detailed the simpler manœuvres, it might be thought that we (as author and publisher) have done all that could be expected of us and that only practice afloat can now complete the novice's initiation. I am, however, a great believer in the power of the written word to teach those who really want to learn and so in this chapter I intend to attempt to describe the real essence of sailing: and for that I would use the word " balance."

Indeed, if we consider any other sport, and most games, it will be realised that the expert practitioner has always a high capacity to use this attribute. The show-jumper flying widely spaced triple bars, the skier in a slalom, the skater poised on the edge of his blade are all engaged in meeting some physical force by the transfer of weight or power. With the possible exception of the horseman (who may or may not be considered as one part of the animal he rides) all—except the glider pilot—operate on a steady platform, the solid earth. The seaman has to perfect his art on water which is frequently ribbed with the moving humps of waves, has beneath him a wedge-shaped hull whose fore and aft axis is actually designed to dip forward and slew to one side as it is heeled, has to correct the trim of his craft in two planes (fore and aft as well as athwartships) at the same time as he adjusts the angle of his sails to the direction of the wind and their size to its force.

Now this is a difficult enough job if there is only one man in the boat. Indeed this is, I think, the great delight of single-handed sailing, for then only your own reactions and sense of balance control the craft. Unfortunately it is virtually impossible for a single-handed sailor to control more than one sail to high perfection, and therefore the classes which cater for him are not many. Most small craft have two sails which, as we have seen, must be more efficient than one, and so we reach the complication that in small unballasted boats the skipper must train a crew to help him achieve balance—which is obviously much more difficult to do than when the whole depends on him alone.

To make any attempt to learn this art from paper it is necessary to take each of the sailor's problems of balance in turn and see if we cannot put down in words the cause of each temporary unbalance and from that deduce the measures to be taken to correct the position.

Let us first take the shape of the hull. In fig. 44 the solid line shows a plan of a small boat's waterline when it is upright and at rest in still water. In the same figure the pecked line shows the theoretical water-line when it is heeled. Two things are at once apparent: when she is heeled there is a great deal more boat in the water on one side than the other, and more of the hull has gone into the water in the after half of the boat than in the forward half.

We are then faced with the same sort of theoretical half-truth that we met in chapter 2, fig. 2, when we discussed only the thwartships effect of heeling and saw how, by the difference of the in and out wedges, a natural stability was built into the boat. For it is obvious that even if the present statement is true the boat will in this hypothesis

140

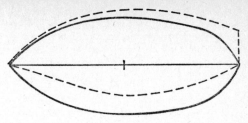

Fig. 44

very quickly do her best to correct the balance of one end against the other and this she will do by dipping her bow and, at the same time, twisting herself towards the heeled side: the twist being helped by the fact that, when so twisted, her keel is now at an angle to her direction of travel and therefore acts as a rudder which will still further increase her attempt to turn into the wind. Within reasonable limits this is not a defect. It is one of the principles which make a boat want to move forward rather than drift sideways, and it is the greatest single safety factor of design—that when she is knocked down by an over-powerful wind she should turn into the gust until she has relieved herself of the too great pressure.

I have said " within reason " because if a boat should continue the turn beyond the control of the helmsman with his rudder she will be so " hard-headed " as to be un-manageable and an obvious danger in crowded anchorages. Her desire to turn can be controlled by the rudder and, as with all adjustments of helm, a little applied early is of far greater benefit than a lot applied later on: of benefit because a large angle of rudder suddenly applied slows a boat very quickly: of benefit because, as a boat's speed drops, the apparent wind draws towards her beam, when it still further increases the heel and the twist.

Of great help, too, in unballasted open boats is the weight-shift of the crew to the high side which, by opposing the heel, helps the boat to return to her normal angle, at once reducing the twisting moment and allowing speed to be regained: and speed regained increases the size of the lee bow-wave which helps to hold the boat's bow up and again reduces her attempt to twist. Conversely, of course, a reduction of speed decreases the wave under the lee bow and so allows the boat to dip and twist. There is nothing which ever happens in a boat which does not affect something else!

As a practical demonstration of how much the fore-and-aft trim of a boat is altered by heeling, it is well worth while to make the following simple experiment with your own craft. First lay her alongside a jetty or pontoon and secure her fore and aft with light lines which should lead to the jetty as nearly as possible at right angles to the centre-line of the boat. Then, taking hold of the shroud or the mast (it is through this spar that the main thrust of the wind is imparted to the boat) you should heel the boat towards you. You will then see the bow dip as she heels and you will see too how the stern line at once goes taut and the bow line slackens as the stem comes towards you.

While rudder application and weight shift at the correct time (which implies that both crew and helmsman are devoting their whole concentration to the job of sailing their boat) provide the obvious corrective, it may well be possible that an incorrectly balanced sail plan will have created an unnatural hard-headedness. The job of choosing the sail to set in varied wind strengths is worth a deal of consideration and experiment, for the answer will not in all classes be the same. In many small lugsail- and gunter-rigged boats a small jib can be carried with a full mainsail; in others a reef in the main must balance a reduction in the size of the jib; while my own ship, with her modern mast-head rig, and by nature a most docile creature, can become very hard-headed unless I take a reef in her main *before* I think of replacing her big jib with a smaller sail. It is up to each captain to find out for himself the attributes of his particular craft.

I have already mentioned the lee bow wave, but this is only one of what we might justly term " the personal waves " of a boat. On the lee, or downwind, side there are two waves, a bow wave and stern wave, and these will be matched on the weather or high side by two similar humps of water which are smaller because, as we have seen from fig. 44 there is much less boat in the water on that side. In effect the boat in her passage through the sea makes for herself a cushion of water which acts as a shock absorber and takes the jerk out of the heeling moment imparted by the wind's gusts. The cushion can act in this way because as the speed increases so do the waves grow larger and offer more support to the hull.

A short study of yachting periodicals (which naturally delight in offering readers pictures of yachts at speed in windy weather) will provide endless opportunities to see the waves of which I speak. From these you will note too, that heavy displacement boats of a deep hull form will show the bow and stern waves in a more sharply defined manner than light displacement boats of shallow form. In fact, when many heavy boats are driven hard there will be seen to be an actual depression in the water between the two waves and that a considerable amount of the yacht's bilge (which would normally be below the water) is now above the line of the sea as it sweeps by her hull.

We have seen that these waves make a cushion for the ship, but it has to be observed that this is a support to the hull which is constantly varying as the speed and the angle of heel alter; and we must recognise that the support is only in a state of balance so long as the heel and the speed are commensurate. If the angle of heel is allowed to increase without an increase in speed there will be no supporting cushion and the ship will fly up into the wind out of control.

It will be seen, therefore, that the experienced sailor (whether he has worked this out for himself or functions from experience) does not, when a gust strikes his ship, immediately let her head go into the wind. He applies rudder firmly and steadily, holds her to her work, maintains the speed, and, if needs must, eases the ship by letting his mainsheet out an inch or two at a time. He does not, except in a real emergency, ease the jibsheet because to do so would be to unbalance the rig, remove a powerful moment which is helping him hold his ship on her course, and greatly reduce the driven power and the speed of the boat.

So far we have only considered these personal waves as cushions supporting the boat when she is heeled, and so have been supposing the ship to be close-hauled or reaching. But the mounds of water are still there when she is running down wind. Then, so long as the boat is upright, the waves on both sides of the hull will be equal—but only so long as the upright position is maintained. As soon as she develops a roll she will (because of her hull form) build up more water on the side to which she leans and this, while it may prevent her going farther that way, will impart a movement which causes her to roll the other way—and so back again—and back again—to be met each time by a vicious tug of the tyro's tiller, making the roll worse.

In these conditions the helmsman must learn to apply rudder *before* the roll has begun and, if someone should suggest that this is like asking that the stable door should be locked before ever the horse has been put in, I would answer that, as with a horseless stable there is a noticeable vacuum! In this case a lack of pressure around the rudder the moment before the roll starts. This feeling of slackness is the warning signal for the application of helm which, if applied at the correct time, need only be comparatively small: an important point because, as always in sail, the use of excess rudder is one of the surest ways of reducing the speed of a boat.

The problem of deciding which way the boat will roll and so which way counter-helm should be applied can be solved by the helmsman's personal sense of balance. I intend to deal with that separately and later in this chapter. For the moment it is enough to note that a steady and early application of rudder can make as great a difference to the comfort of those aboard a little ship running down wind as it can increase the speed of her progress.

We have, too, while we are thinking of our vessel as travelling down wind, to consider once again the effect of the balance of the sails, and never more so than when from the wind's strength there is an obvious need to reduce the amount of canvas she carries. In light weather if the main can be balanced by a spinnaker or a boomed-out jib the steering will be greatly eased. In heavy weather the main should be reefed before the jib and in very strong winds taken in altogether so that the vessel runs under head sails only.

Mention of hard weather introduces the problem of the waves other than those made by the ship herself—the real waves of the sea. These should always be considered as separate from the personal waves created by the ship, and indeed by comparison they are enormous mounds of water. When she is close hauled or reaching, the same cushion of personal waves can be found for her support—so long as her speed is maintained. The latter is a vital point. It is true that when reaching or headed into the sea the personal waves meeting the true waves may create a lot of spray which will be blown back against the ship and over her people. But spray hurts no one who is prepared for it. If you are to retain momentum to climb or break through the true waves it is imperative that speed is maintained. The ship must be sailed hard all the time, the sails kept full, and the brake of the rudder applied as little as possible.

But down wind, or with a quartering sea, the position is different. Then we are, in effect, running away from the true waves without any chance of escaping—for no sailing ship ever built has outstripped waves whose crests travel at something over 30 knots. What matters is that the water in these seas (where they are large) is in a very delicate state of balance. Waves can be greatly upset and made to break dangerously either by an adverse tide running into the sea or by the shoaling of the sea's bed. They can also be made to break by their meeting with the fanned-out wake of a ship's personal waves—even those from a vessel as small as that which we are considering in this book. Then, even if the break is not as big as it would have been if the ship had been larger, it will at least be large in comparison with the ship whose passage has caused the break.

So here again we are faced with a problem of balance: to go, as it were, on tip-toe through the angry waters so that we escape the fury of a breaking crest. Observe the sea closely in heavy weather and see that the so-called white horses will, in deep water and when there is no strong current, slide down the back of the wave the moment the spume has broken. If they can be kept like this they are harmless. And the best way of keeping them so is (after you have decided to stay in deep water and away from tidal rips) to reduce the personal waves of the boat to the very minimum, which means simply this: it is unlikely in really bad weather that a small ship will be able to go to windward at all. She must reach or run for some known shelter under reduced canvas.

So we see that a very great deal is going to depend all the time, good weather or bad, on the helmsman's personal sense of balance, for only this will keep him continuously advised of the varied forces acting upon the craft he steers; and the more surely and the more immediately he can make the ship pass on to him what the wind and sea are doing to her, the more quickly will he come to her help with tiller or sheet. If this sense of balance is more deeply vested in some people than in others it is yet quite certain that the physical attitude adopted by the helmsman can largely determine his ability to measure the forces that act on his boat. Or, looking at the matter in another way, he must learn to identify himself so completely with the ship he sails that a blow struck at her is felt as a direct attack on his own body.

There would appear to be two ways of achieving this. One is, with feet and thighs, to so jam yourself into the cockpit or sternsheets that you feel every tremor of the ship; and the other to position yourself so that your body can move freely in every direction, when the necessary balancing act keeps you continually advised of the stresses imposed on your boat. Which of these positions to choose must surely be up to the individual helmsman, and the choice when made is purely a question of temperament. If I myself very much prefer the more flexible position of balance it is probably because I derive real enjoyment from the more delicate sensation.

Once you have your body going with the ship there is no fear of being flung overboard by a sudden lurch. You have one hand on the tiller and the other resting lightly on the gunwale or cockpit coaming. In very bad weather I prefer that the hand which is available for support should hold not to any wood of the ship but to a rope hand-grip which can be made by a bow-hitch with any available rope (the ends of the mainsheet or one of the jib sheets). Then only my bottom and feet will be in direct contact with the hull and, as every schoolboy knows, the posterior is an extremely sensitive part!

Even with ships large enough to be steered by a wheel I think the stance adopted should still be light and flexible rather than heavy and fixed. Then, with feet wide enough apart to counter the roll, the weight of the body is poised on the balls of the feet so that the heels are used only to steady the body in its state of balance: if an extra support be needed a length of line can be passed round the helmsman's waist so that he may have something against which to lean back. The big point to note is that, whether seated beside a tiller or standing before a wheel to achieve balance, once the rhythm of the ship has been found this is less tiring than to jam yourself solid. The experienced sailor goes with the movement of his ship, he never willingly fights it.

Watch the passengers on the decks of a liner in bad weather. They rush slitheringly from side to side while their feet beat the deck in their hectic efforts to counter the move of the ship. But see one of the crew pass through them. He will pause, wait until the ship is going his way, and then let her help his feet until, at the end of the rhythm, he must pause again: a series of unhurried forward movements in a straight line punctuated by spells when he must wait. The same choice of the moment to move is even more important in a small boat.

We must (having, I hope, made this point about personal balance) now go back to the problem of steering a boat down wind in a seaway. As a wave overtakes the boat the stern is lifted, the bow depressed. The stern-wave is thereby reduced in size at the same time that the bow wave is greatly increased. If the boat is dead before the sea and is upright she may be expected to ride easily forward on the twin and enlarged cushions of the bow wave.

But, if she is heeled or if she has presented her quarter to the sea, then the lee bow wave will be the only one of the four cushions left and that one large mound of water will be doing its best to push the boat's bow round and to turn her broadside to the seas in such a way that the next sea may, by reason of the disturbance she has caused in turning, break aboard her.

And here a motor boat, despite her engine, is just as likely to be proved vulnerable unless her helmsman is alive to what is happening beneath him. In the top of a big wave the water is often " soft " and frothy and can offer little resistance either to a propeller or to a rudder both of which are necessarily not far below the surface. It will be seen, therefore, how important it is that you should have firmly fixed within your body both the rhythm of the ship as she heels to the wind and the other rhythm imparted by the seas through which she moves. As a pianist may be called upon to play a different time with each hand and yet produce a phonic answer, so the two rhythms must be controlled by the tiller and one never allowed to outbalance the other. When the rhythms are known and appreciated, rudder may be applied before ever the position of un-balance is reached. Then the boat will be held steadily to her work and the helmsman will recognise the true delight of sailing a little ship in a big sea.

We have said often enough in this book that much can be learnt from the written word—and so it can. But the discovery of these rhythmic balances must be left to the individual going out in his ship to the sea. No written word can help his inexperience beyond this point. Only his desire to perfect himself will open the doors to him. No one, however good his theory might be, would expect to play a piano without practice. It is the same with boats. Book-learning may help the start of your journey. Where you finish is up to you.

CHAPTER 14

The different characteristics of inboard and outboard installations—
The outboard is also the rudder—The full outboard motor boat the
most difficult of all craft to handle—Used as an auxiliary it is better
to mount the outboard engine to one side and retain the rudder—
Speed is expensive in fuel—Simple hydrodynamics of propeller
propulsion—Trim can be corrected by altering the angle of the
engine relative to the transom.

A very great deal of what I have written may appear to
have been directed to the sailing as opposed to the
" motoring " men, although much will have equal force
for the man who prefers to trust himself only to mechan-
ical power. His desire for a naturally stable hull in
which to embark his family are the same, the method of
launching from a trailer is similar, and his need to understand the charts, buoyage and tides will be equal to that
of his sail-minded friend. If, in reading this book, the
motor-boat man should learn something of the problems
of sail, so much the better. He will have more under-
standing for his fellow seafarer.

On the other side of the coin, the sailing man may
well decide to equip himself with an outboard engine, if
only that he may return to the slipway in time to put his
boat on the trailer before the tide is too low, or merely to
increase the allowable radius of his sailing. So no apology
is made for closing this book with a chapter on engines,
particularly those of the outboard variety.

The difference between inboard and outboard is not only
a question of the greater cost of the inboard-engined boat.
The latter engine is still a great deal heavier than an outboard of similar performance and the weight may not, as
in an outboard, be easily divorced from the weight of the

boat if the job of getting her on to her trailer should prove unusually difficult. There are other considerations. We have agreed that sooner or later, playing about in the creeks and harbours, we shall go aground. Most outboard engines are fitted with a release which allows the engine to swing up, and when it does so many of the larger ones will switch themselves off. An inboard boat, unless it is fitted with a fairly deep false keel or a skeg, will damage the propeller and bend the shaft—an expensive job to put right and an accident which entails rowing the boat home.

Against these advantages we have to realise that an outboard engine will in most cases be the rudder as well as the driving force, and so, when the engine is put into neutral there will be no means left of steering the boat until the clutch is again engaged. This makes the full outboard motor-boat the most difficult of all craft to handle in a seamanlike manner. Which is worth noting because the general public, probably because of the similarity to motor-cars, seem to think that this type of craft offers the simplest means of getting afloat.

The man buying a small sailing boat, and using an engine only as an auxiliary, would be well advised to keep his rudder shipped and to have the engine so fitted that it will be to one side of the rudder fittings. The man with the fully-powered outboard motor-boat will not, of course, wish to adopt this way out. He will have to learn how to handle the craft: to come alongside a jetty by using short bursts of power applied with the engine at a pre-set angle to the hull—either ahead or astern.

The powers developed by a large outboard are very great. In the first range they vary from the big six-cylinder " X " class sports models of near 100 horse power down to 25 horse power. These are all suitable for water ski-ing if fitted to a hull which has been designed for high speed

151

work. Thereafter, coming down the horse power scale, there are 18, 12 and 10 horse power models for pushing cruisers and work-boats, and finally smaller ones for day-sailers down to those of minimal power for propelling little pram dinghies. The whole field is covered and it only remains for you to decide which is the best for your purpose and purse.

But here a warning. Speed on the water, as indeed speed anywhere else, is expensive to obtain both in first cost and in the consumption of fuel. When the thrust has to be imparted by a propeller working in water, the expenditure of fuel will rise even more steeply than the indicated horse power might suggest. High-speed outboards are great fun to drive, but the petrol bill at the end of a holiday can be a horrid shock.

Considering, then, the application of a medium-size outboard to a " displacement " hull for fishing and pottering about, or when used as an auxiliary to a boat normally propelled by sails, we have to realise that some adjustment must be made to our normal sailing trim, and some adjustment made to the angle of the engine to suit the particular boat.

When power is applied to the stern of a boat and she begins to move fast through the water her stern is sucked down by the paddle wheel effect of the rotating propeller, and by the fact that the boat's stern tries to fill the furrow in the water created by the passage of her own mid-section. It will be seen, then, why craft designed for high speed have a stern which is quite different from that of any other type of vessel. This means (see fig. 45) that your type of boat may try to travel as in A. If she does you will have to do something about it, because she will then not only be tending to become unstable, but she will be setting up a fearsome drag wave which is going to make you most unpopular in the anchorage.

152

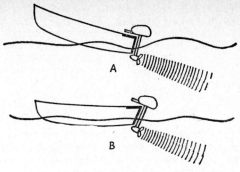

Fig. 45

Even if it be a rather unsociable way out of the difficulty, you can move your passengers forward. It does, however, point to the desirability of stowing as much as possible of the heavy gear forward, and gear can be very heavy. Just try stopping the car on the way to the sea at a railway station and have all the gear weighed that you and your family intend to take aboard. If your family is anything like mine the clobber they carry may well total more than a hundredweight.

It is better to correct the trim by altering the rake of the engine. Nearly all outboards have adjustable brackets. If, as in fig. 45B, the propeller can be directed downwards, the altered line of thrust in relation to the boat can be made to lift the stern and depress the bow. This is without, you will notice, any marked effect on the angle of the thrust into the water, because, though we shall have canted the engine, we shall have altered the trim of the boat by approximately the same angle. We shall also have cut down the drag wave, appreciably added to the boat's speed and,

153

because the hull will be nearer to its correct fore and aft trim, we shall have regained a great deal of her natural stability.

For various reasons the maximum angle at which we can set the engine is somewhere near 12 degrees from the vertical. If we reach 15 degrees and still have not obtained a clean running wake astern of the boat we have to face the fact that we are trying to drive this particular hull too fast. In other words the boat is over-engined, and if we want a peaceful ride in a good sea-boat we shall be well advised to change the engine for one of less power—and greater economy.

Index

(Illustrations indicated by asterisk)